# 150 NATURE HOT SPOTS IN CALIFORNIA

## The Best Parks, Conservation Areas and Wild Places

Ann Marie Brown

FIREFLY BOOKS

Published by Firefly Books Ltd. 2019


First printing

Library of Congress Control Number: 2018961489

Library and Archives Canada Cataloguing in Publication
Brown, Ann Marie, author
150 nature hot spots in California : the best parks, conservation areas and wild places / Ann Marie Brown.
Includes index.
ISBN 978-0-228-10168-0 (softcover)
1. Natural areas--California--Guidebooks. 2. Parks--California--Guidebooks. 3. Protected areas--California--Guidebooks. 4. California--Description and travel. 5. California--Guidebooks. 6. Guidebooks.
I. Title. II. Title: One hundred fifty nature hot spots in California.
F859.3.B66 2019 917.9404 C2018-905975-3

Published in the United States by
Firefly Books (U.S.) Inc.
P.O. Box 1338, Ellicott Station
Buffalo, New York 14205

Published in Canada by
Firefly Books Ltd.
50 Staples Avenue, Unit 1
Richmond Hill, Ontario L4B 0A7

Cover and interior design: Hartley Millson

Printed in China

## Acknowledgments

A big thank-you goes to the many park rangers, naturalists, public information officers and volunteers who aided me in my research and advised me in fact-checking this book. These dedicated people took time out of their busy schedules to patiently answer my questions and offer valuable comments, suggestions and corrections. (Any errors in these pages are entirely mine.) Also, a special thanks to Steve Cameron and the wonderful people at Firefly Books, who provided me with this opportunity and turned my words and images into a book.

# Contents

**Nature Hot Spots and Dogs**
Given the delicate nature of many of these destinations, we strongly recommend that you leave your pets at home. Even the most well-behaved dogs are capable of disrupting a sensitive ecosystem, and their presence and excrement may scare animals away, which could affect your wildlife-watching experience. If you wish to bring your dog, please contact the destination in advance to learn about limitations and any precautions you must take. Please obey all signs, dispose of your pet's excrement appropriately and take additional care when meeting other people and pets.

**Universal Access**
Many websites for the selected destinations will provide information regarding universal access. Please note that this information may refer to specific trails, parking or toilets at the hot spots, and visitors with accessibility needs may be unable to fully experience the highlights described in this book. Please confirm the availability of accessible facilities and trails prior to departure.

# Introduction

A wise person once said that a culture can be measured by the resources it chooses to protect. If that's true, then California's preserved lands are a lofty credit to American culture. Despite being one of the country's most populous states, California is blessed with a wealth of protected wild land. Within the state's borders are 28 units of America's National Park system, 36 National Natural Landmarks, nine designated Wild and Scenic Rivers, two World Heritage Sites and 280 state parks. Additionally, California boasts 149 federally designated Wilderness areas — huge tracts of undeveloped land that comprise about 15 percent of the state.

These preserved lands celebrate California's remarkably diverse terrain, which includes 24,000 square miles of desert, 33 million acres of forest, nearly 1,200 miles of Pacific coastline, a bounty of snow-capped peaks and alpine lakes, a smattering of islands and even a handful of volcanoes.

It's a landscape of breathtaking extremes, where superlatives abound. Among California's long list of chart-toppers, Mount Whitney sets the bar as the highest peak in the contiguous United States (14,505 feet in elevation). Less than 150 miles away, Death Valley's Badwater holds the record as the lowest point in the western hemisphere at 282 feet below sea level. Other record holders include El Capitan, the world's largest single piece of granite; Yosemite Falls, North America's tallest waterfall; and Mount Shasta, the largest stratovolcano in the Cascade Range, which spans from California to British Columbia.

In the flora category, California is home to the largest, the oldest

and the tallest. The state is the only place in the world where the world's largest living trees, the giant sequoias, grow. California's arid, eastern side is home to the planet's oldest living things, the ancient bristlecone pines. The state's wetter, northern reaches support massive groves of the world's tallest living things, the coast redwoods.

California is rich in fauna too. Massive Roosevelt elk wander among the Northwest's redwood groves. Bighorn sheep clatter across rocky slopes above the desert canyons. From December to April, Pacific gray whales pass by on their annual 10,000-mile migration. In the summer, blue whales and humpbacks feed in coastal waters. Cuddly sea otters float among the kelp beds. California condors soar over the Coast Range, their wings stretching 10 feet wide. Salmon wriggle upstream to spawn in the same waters where they were born. Monarch butterflies overwinter in eucalyptus groves. Herds of pronghorn antelope graze in grassland prairies.

The 150 nature hot spots described in this book can lead you to many of California's greatest marvels. These are some of my favorite places on earth, and I hope everyone gets the chance to feel their awe. But this wish comes with a caveat: please tread lightly and reverently as you travel. Despite its seemingly endless riches, the natural world is fragile. Do what you can to protect it.

I wish you many inspiring days on the trail.

– Ann Marie Brown

These icons appear throughout to give you an idea of the available activities and features at each hot spot:

- **Hiking**
- **Camping**
- **Wildlife viewing**
- **Plantlife viewing**
- **Historical or cultural site**
- **Cycling**
- **Stargazing**
- **Spelunking and cave exploration**
- **Rock climbing**
- **Beach exploration and tide pools**
- **Kayaking, canoeing or rafting**
- **Swimming**
- **Scuba diving or snorkeling**
- **Surfing**
- **Skiing or snowboarding**
- **Snowshoeing**
- **Fishing**

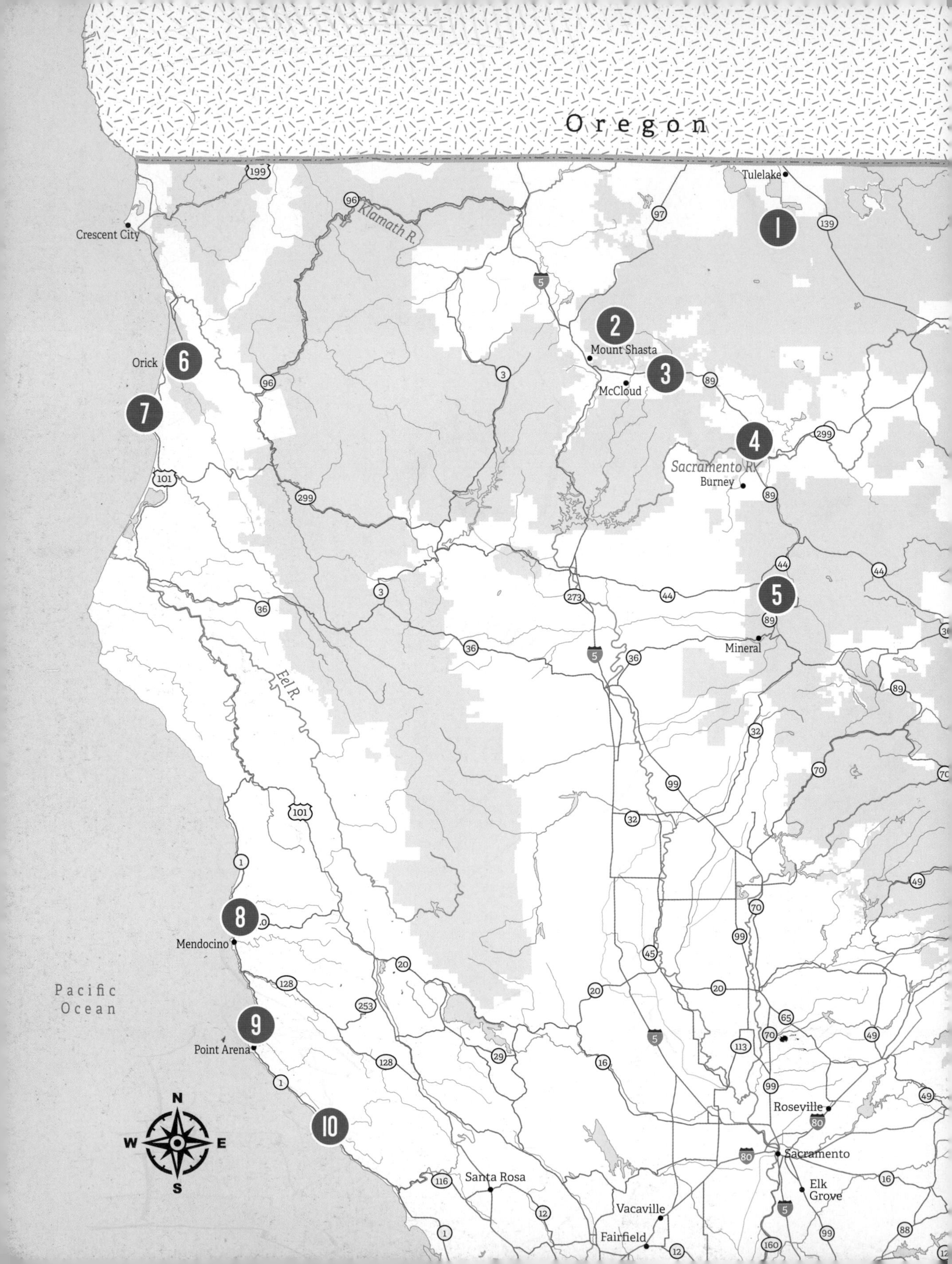

Oregon
Tulelake
Crescent City
Klamath R.
Mount Shasta
McCloud
Orick
Sacramento R.
Burney
Mineral
Eel R.
Mendocino
Pacific Ocean
Point Arena
Roseville
Sacramento
Santa Rosa
Elk Grove
Vacaville
Fairfield
N
S
E
W

# Northern California

# Lava Beds National Monument

***A surreal landscape sculpted by molten earth***

### Hot Spot Highlights

- Tunnel through lava tube caves.
- Visit the site of the 1870s Modoc War.
- See 4,000-year-old Native American petroglyphs and pictographs.

**Address**: Lava Beds National Monument, 1 Indian Well Headquarters, Tulelake, CA
**Tel.**: (530) 667-8113
**Website**: www.nps.gov/labe

**Best season:**
October to April (when it's coolest)

! Observe heat warnings in the summer

↗ **The tailless pika is known for making hay while the sun shines — collecting grasses in summer to store for food in the winter.**

Lava Beds National Monument's volcanic tablelands are punctuated by cinder cones, pit craters, spatter cones and more than 700 lava tube caves. Its sagebrush-covered plains and lava flows are dotted with mountain mahogany and western junipers, creating habitat for mule deer, pronghorns, rabbits and a multitude of birds. For thousands of years this land was home to the Modoc Indian tribes, who left behind a legacy of ancient petroglyphs and pictographs.

After the snow melts in spring, Lava Beds comes alive with wildflowers — bright pink sagebrush mariposa lilies, red desert Indian paintbrush, yellow blazing star and six different species of brilliant blue penstemon. The blooming period is staggered between March and August, so flower seekers can usually find some color most of the spring and summer.

In summer, the lava fields may be uncomfortably hot, so visitors seek shelter in the lava tube caves, where the temperature is always mild, sometimes even chilly. With a flashlight or headlamp and loose, layered clothes, you can explore the caves on your own — no spelunking experience is needed. And although you don't cover much ground quickly, you may still get a workout: you will duck, twist and crawl as

you navigate through these intriguing volcanic features.

Wildlife watchers will find a wide variety of creatures in Lava Beds. While exploring the caves, you may be lucky enough to spot a cave cricket, a rubber boa or one of 14 different species of bats. Outside the caves, herds of mule deer are commonly seen, as well as black-tailed jackrabbits and the charming American pika, a tiny member of the rabbit family that looks more like a tailless mouse. The pika needs cool weather to survive, so it lives in the rocks of the caves and cave collapse areas.

Birders might spot the brilliant blue lazuli bunting or the melodic western meadowlark. Stop at the West and East Wildlife Overlooks to see resident and migratory birds, especially waterfowl, at Tule Lake.

In addition to its compelling geology, wildlife and cultural history, Lava Beds was also

**↑ More than 700 lava tube caves beckon visitors to explore, but you'll need a flashlight or headlamp to light your path.**

**↖ Lava Beds' vivid wildflower show includes wild blue flax, or *linum lewisii*, which grows up to 2 feet tall.**

the site of the only major Native American war fought in California. In 1872, the federal government tried to remove a band of Modoc Indians from this land. By hiding among the lava beds' wide trenches, rock outcrops and small caves, 52 Modocs held off some 600 government troops for nearly 5 months. Walk the 2-mile Captain Jack's Stronghold Trail to learn the story. And while your boots are laced, hike the 0.75-mile trail to the Schonchin Butte fire lookout tower, perched on the monument's highest peak at 5,302 feet.

Lava Beds is located in a remote area, so load up on gasoline, snacks and water. The park has only one campground, Indian Well, located near the visitor center and Cave Loop Road. The nearby town of Tulelake has motels, restaurants and grocery stores.

## Cave Loop Road

The most popular caves at Lava Beds are the two dozen lava tubes found on the Cave Loop Road near the visitor center. These are considered "developed" caves, which means they have well-marked trails, stairs or ladders. The caves are rated for difficulty, and first-time cave explorers should start out with "easy" caves that have high ceilings and smooth floors, like Big Painted Cave, Valentine Cave and Symbol Bridge. Mushpot Cave is the only lighted cave at Lava Beds, and its educational exhibits are great for first-time visitors. If you're comfortable in these caves, move on to longer, more challenging ones like Hopkins Chocolate Cave (1,405 feet long) or Blue Grotto Cave (1,541 feet long). These involve more stooping and crawling. A good flashlight is key to your enjoyment — not only to help you find your way but also so you can see the caves' year-round ice, colorful lichens, shimmery minerals, and features such as pillars, benches, falls and cascades. For an even greater challenge, visit Catacombs Cave, one of the longest and most complex, with a total length of 6,903 feet and numerous forks, twists and turns.

## Petroglyph Point

Don't miss making a trip to Petroglyph Point in the park's northeastern reaches to see some of more than 5,000 carvings or petroglyphs left by multiple generations of Modoc Indians. This extensive series of geometric shapes is considered to be California's greatest concentration of ancient Native American art. The carvings date back at least 2,000 years and are found on a tall cliff that was once an island in vast Tule Lake, which was drained for agriculture in the 20th century. The Modoc must have travelled by canoe to make their carvings in the soft volcanic tuff. Visitors can hike past the artwork (the carvings are protected by a tall fence), then climb to the top of the point for views of Medicine Lake Volcano and the surrounding basin.

You can also see Native American pictographs (drawings) near some of the lava tube cave entrances, including Symbol Bridge and Big Painted Cave. On summer Saturdays, rangers lead guided tours to Fern Cave, where Native American art decorates the walls. The cave is also home to many rare ferns and plants. Make reservations in advance for this special tour at www.recreation.gov, as self-guided hikes are not permitted.

**↑ Native American petroglyphs, some more than 20 centuries old, can be viewed at Petroglyph Point.**

**← Lava tubes are great insulators. Heppe Ice Cave contains seasonal ice formations that melt to create a chilly pool in the summer.**

**↙ Moist, cool cave air creates fog at the entrance to Valentine Cave.**

# Mount Shasta

***A mighty snow-capped volcano reigns over the Northern California landscape***

## Hot Spot Highlights

- Hire a guide for the epic trek to the top of the Cascades' largest stratovolcano.
- Wander through subalpine meadows to see a sacred natural spring and colorful wildflowers.
- Hike to the summits of Gray Butte and Black Butte, Shasta's close neighbors.

**Address**: Mount Shasta Ranger Station, 204 West Alma, Mt. Shasta, CA
**Tel.**: (530) 926-4511
**Website**: www.fs.usda.gov/detail/stnf/home/?cid=stelprdb5339074

**Best season:**
June to October

**↗ Majestic bald eagles, with wingspans of up to eight feet, fish for trout in the lakes near Mount Shasta.**

**→ Mount Shasta sees its mirror image in the tranquil waters of tiny Heart Lake.**

Mount Shasta soars to 14,179 feet high and can be seen from 150 miles away on clear days. It's not California's highest peak — that's Mount Whitney at 14,505 feet — although its prodigious height puts it in the top five. What sets this mountain apart is its hulking volume. Shasta has a massive base diameter of 17 miles, and a total volume of 85 cubic miles. It's the largest stratovolcano in the Cascades, a range that spans from California to British Columbia. The dormant volcanic cone sits solo on the horizon, rising majestically 5,000 feet above its tallest neighbor, Black Butte.

California poet Joaquin Miller described Mount Shasta as "lone as God and white as a winter's moon." The whiteness varies with the season, but even in summer the mountain has a permanent cap of ice and snow. Runoff from its glaciers feed dozens of waterways, most importantly the McCloud, Shasta and Sacramento rivers. Shasta's glaciers include four of California's largest — the Whitney and Bolam glaciers on its north side, and the Hotlum and Wintun glaciers on its east side. But these glaciers

↑ **Sweeping lenticular clouds frame the summit of Mount Shasta about 60 days per year.**

may be short-lived — if Mount Shasta erupts, the ensuing lava and mud flows would likely eliminate them. The peak last erupted in 1786, and some scientists predict it may soon erupt again. Shasta is high on the United States Geological Survey's list of California's "highest-threat volcanoes."

The volcano is known for creating its own weather, which can change at a moment's notice. Mount Shasta is so massive, high and solitary that it disrupts the air currents around it. Oddly shaped lenticular clouds form near its summit about 60 days per year, most commonly in fall and winter, and even on the clearest days. The clouds, which look like stacks of pancakes, appear to be sitting motionless, but they are actually rushing streams of condensed moisture. Experienced Shasta hikers know the rule: never attempt to summit the mountain when you can

↑ **From Bunny Flat, Mount Shasta's summit seems deceptively close.**

see a lenticular. When a storm moves in, it can last for days, with little or no visibility.

From Mount Shasta city, Everitt Memorial Highway rises 15 miles up Shasta's slopes, giving drivers easy access to the 7,900-foot elevation level. A popular trailhead lies at Bunny Flat (6,860 feet), just above timberline. Here, groves of red fir and pines give way to volcanic rubble, scree, and icy snow. In the summer months, drivers can proceed a few miles farther uphill to Everitt Vista Point (7,900 feet) for exceptional views of Shasta, plus Mount Eddy and the Marble Mountains to the west, and Lassen Peak to the south.

## Summiting Mount Shasta

The idea of summiting Mount Shasta appeals to many hikers' sense of adventure. More than 15,000 summit attempts are made every year, and only a third are successful. Most people attempt it between May and July, when there's still enough snow on the southern slopes to make footholds easier. When the snow melts, patches of loose ash and cinder appear, making the climbing harder and increasing the chance of a rockfall.

Although some hardy climbers make the exhausting 10-hour ascent — plus a 5-hour descent — in one day, typically starting at 2 a.m. from Bunny Flat, most break it into 2 days, with a night spent at Horse Camp (7,900 feet). Various routes lead to the summit, but the easiest and most popular scales the south and west sides of Shasta via Avalanche Gulch, with a breathtaking and thigh-burning 7,300-foot elevation gain. The route usually requires crampons, an ice ax and a helmet, plus a summit permit from the Mount Shasta Ranger Station. First-timers should go with a knowledgeable guide (a shop called The Fifth Season in Mount Shasta city rents climbing equipment and offers guided

↑ **The curved trunks of hemlocks are a testament to Mount Shasta's heavy winter snow.**

climbs). In late summer, some hikers opt for the Clear Creek route up the mountain's east side. By August, this summit route is usually snow-free.

Much easier day-hikes are also popular on Mount Shasta. From Bunny Flat, casual hikers can walk 2 miles to Shasta Alpine Lodge at Horse Camp. The stone lodge was built by the Sierra Club in 1923, and it houses exhibits on Mount Shasta and a small library of mountaineering books. During the late May through September climbing season, Horse Camp is staffed by knowledgeable caretakers.

## Gray Butte

A few miles farther up the road, a small campground and trailhead is found at Panther Meadows, and another is located farther uphill at the Old Ski Hill parking area. From Panther Meadows Campground, the summit of Gray Butte is a first-rate hike, offering unforgettable views of Mount Shasta, especially at

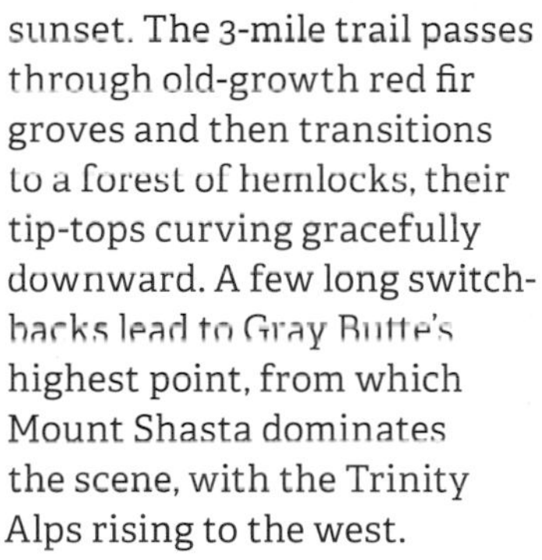

sunset. The 3-mile trail passes through old-growth red fir groves and then transitions to a forest of hemlocks, their tip-tops curving gracefully downward. A few long switchbacks lead to Gray Butte's highest point, from which Mount Shasta dominates the scene, with the Trinity Alps rising to the west.

## Panther Meadows

Another fine hike travels through gorgeous Panther Meadows, two small subalpine meadows that are fed by a natural spring. Members of the Wintu Indian tribe revere the spring and consider the meadows sacred — they still perform ceremonies here, as they have for thousands of years. Start from the upslope trailhead at Old Ski Hill, or the downslope trailhead at Panther Meadows Campground — the trail runs between the two. In the summer months, the meadow grasses are peppered with pink heathers, red paintbrush, purple asters and other delicate wildflowers. (Visit in late July to see the flowers in their full glory.) The snow-streaked peak of Mount Shasta looms over the meadows, standing in bold contrast to the blue sky.

**↑ Some of Panther Meadows' diminutive mountain heathers — identified by their tiny bell-shaped flowers — are more than a century old.**

**↑↑ Shasta buckwheat comes in many colors and forms, including this bi-color pink and cream.**

**↖ The tubular blooms of purple penstemon brighten Mount Shasta's gritty volcanic soil.**

**↑ Western tanagers flash their fiery plumage as they fly through the deep green of Shasta's red fir forests.**

**↑↑ The stream that flows through Panther Meadows is bordered by delicate mosses and grasses.**

**→ On the mountain's lower slopes, red firs and hemlocks thrive in Shasta's rock-strewn soil.**

## Black Butte

Mount Shasta has a close neighbor, and it offers astounding views of the massive volcano. From its base, 6,325-foot Black Butte looks impossibly steep, its nearly treeless cone of andesite looming 2,400 feet above Interstate 5. But gaining the summit of this jagged plug dome volcano is easier than it looks via a 5.2-mile round-trip hike. The trail leads through a fir and pine forest to a rocky talus slope on Black Butte's north side, then curves around the mountain until views of 14,179-foot Mount Shasta open wide, framed by Shasta Valley and the mountains of Oregon beyond. Shasta demands your attention, but don't neglect the westward vista of Mount Eddy and the Klamath Range. On the summit, a narrow ledge leads to the square foundation of an old fire-lookout tower. Guides from Mount Shasta Ranger District lead full-moon hikes on select evenings each summer, or you can hike on your own (day or night) from May to November, when Black Butte is snow-free.

**↑ To drivers on Interstate 5, the cone of monolithic Black Butte looms large, but when viewed from the shores of Castle Lake, it's dwarfed by neighboring Mount Shasta.**

# McCloud Falls

***A trio of waterfalls on the McCloud River creates a misty playground for hikers, swimmers and anglers***

## Hot Spot Highlights

- Drive the McCloud River Loop and stop to visit three waterfall overlooks.
- Hike the shady riverside trail to see the waterfalls up close.
- Fish for trout in the prime fly-fishing waters of the McCloud River.

**Address**: Hwy 89 between Fowlers Camp and Cattle Camp, McCloud, CA
**Tel.**: (530) 964-2184
**Website**: https://mountshastatrailassociation.org

**Best season:**
April to October

↗ **The water ouzel, or American dipper, is remarkably well adapted to life by the river — it's as comfortable traveling in water as it is in air.**

↗↗ **Handsome Steller's jays are common companions in the dense conifer forest bordering the McCloud River, and they also frequent the nearby campgrounds.**

In the shadow of mighty Mount Shasta, a trio of waterfalls drops on the McCloud River, its water born of glacial ice and alpine snows. Shaped by the same volcanic forces that created Mount Shasta, the energetic river has carved a channel through a deep canyon that contains lava flows, talus basalt jumbles, and cliffs composed of tufa. The falls were formed where the flowing river encountered erosion-resistant bands of basalt.

Of the three McCloud waterfalls, graceful Middle Falls is the scene-stealer, with its commanding 50-foot wall of water plunging over a basalt cliff. A cacophonous, watery roar fills your ears long before you see its splashing spray. Wider than it is tall, the misty cataract is split in two by a rocky buttress crowned with the large, deep-green leaves of Indian rhubarb. Water ouzels build their homes behind the waterfall's curtain; watch carefully and you may spot this remarkable aquatic songbird flying in or out of the spray. Also called the American dipper, the ouzel can actually swim underwater by propelling itself with powerful strokes of its wings.

Tucked into a narrow slot between basalt columns, 15-foot-high Lower Falls is a popular put-in spot for kayakers paddling the McCloud River and for summer visitors looking to cool off in its deep pool (cliff jumping is popular here). Chattering gray squirrels and noisy Steller's jays frequent the area, hoping for handouts

↑ **Middle McCloud Falls is framed by old-growth firs and ponderosa pines.**

from picnickers. (Keep them wild — don't feed them.)

Upper McCloud Falls is the most secluded of the three — its narrow funnel drops into a circular, seafoam-green pool, nearly hidden from the trail. In spring and early summer, sheets of swirling mist drift downstream. A picnic area nearby provides a pleasant spot for lunch or a rest.

To access the falls, drive the McCloud River Loop, which starts at Cattle Camp on Highway 89. The 6-mile paved road provides parking access for all three waterfalls, plus a swimming hole at Cattle Camp. If you'd rather hike than drive, start at the Lower Falls Picnic Area parking lot (near Fowlers Campground) and walk the 3.8-mile riverside trail. The stretch near Lower McCloud Falls is paved and wheelchair accessible; the path turns to dirt shortly beyond Fowlers Camp. Large, old-growth fir trees, interspersed with ponderosa pines and dogwoods, create a shady canopy. Keep an eye out for occasional Pacific yew trees, easily identified by their red, peeling bark.

Fly-fishermen can try their luck on the McCloud River, which is stocked with rainbow, German brown, and brook trout. Many prefer the riffles and rapids above and below Middle and Lower Falls. The river stretch below Lower Falls is California's only fishery that supports Dolly Varden trout, a member of the char family and a state-listed endangered species.

# McArthur-Burney Falls Memorial State Park

***A spring-fed waterfall cascades over volcanic rock into a mossy basin***

## Hot Spot Highlights

- Marvel at one of California's most superb waterfalls, which pours from both above and within the cliff face.
- Fish in Burney Creek or Lake Britton.
- Birdwatch for bald eagles and black swifts.

**Address:** McArthur-Burney Falls State Park, 24898 Hwy 89, Burney, CA
**Tel.:** (530) 335-2777
**Websites:** www.parks.ca.gov/?page_id=455, www.burneyfallspark.org

**Best season:**
Year-round

**↗ Basalt rocks near Burney Falls are draped in thick, green moss, owing to the ever-present mist billowing off the falls.**

At 129 feet, Burney Falls is nowhere near the tallest waterfall in California, but its claims to fame are its photogenic beauty and remarkable reliability. The misty marvel gushes 100 million gallons of turquoise water at nearly the exact same rate every day — no matter whether it's dry summer season or wet winter season. Legend has it that President Teddy Roosevelt loved this waterfall; he is said to have called it "the eighth wonder of the world."

A product of the same volcanic region that created Mount Shasta and Mount Lassen, Burney Creek's water sources are underground springs and snowmelt stored in basalt rock layers, over which the waterfall pours. Much of its flow actually pours *out* of the cliff face — it's siphoned through tiny basalt crevices — rather than plummeting over its lip. Because these water droplets have just emerged from the cool

underground, Burney Creek's milky-blue pool is a chilly 42 degrees Fahrenheit even on the warmest summer days.

You can see Burney Falls with a quick drive into the park and a short walk to the waterfall overlook, but that would mean missing out on this park's other wonders. Instead, walk a loop to and around the waterfall: from the park's main trailhead, go left on the Headwaters Trail, heading upstream and away from the falls. The woods are filled with huge Douglas firs

and ponderosa pines (easily identified by their clearly delineated, jigsaw-puzzle bark), plus white oaks and black oaks. Black basalt rocks seem to completely cover every inch of bare ground. Many are coated with thick moss from the waterfall's constant mist. In half a mile, join the Pacific Crest Trail where it crosses Burney Creek. Cross the long footbridge and follow the PCT to the Falls Loop Trail junction. Follow Falls Loop back to your car.

As you wander, keep on the lookout for a few special bird species that frequent this park: migratory black swifts, which build their nests on the waterfall's sheer cliffs in early summer; and bald eagles and osprey, which nest at nearby Lake Britton. The lake is a fisherman's paradise, filled with trout, black bass, crappie and catfish. Boat, kayak and canoe rentals are available. Many anglers also fish Burney Creek above the falls, where there are both wild and stocked trout.

If you want to stay overnight, the park's campground has 121 forested sites and 24 insulated cabins. The nearest lodgings are found in the small town of Burney.

**↑ One hundred million gallons of water pour over Burney Falls every day, constantly refilling its cobalt blue pool.**

**↖ Looking like a masked clown with a bright red cap, the acorn woodpecker gathers acorns from the park's oak trees.**

# Lassen Volcanic National Park

***A marvelous conglomeration of volcanic and hydrothermal features***

## Hot Spot Highlights

- Hike to the top of a dormant volcano.
- Marvel at bubbling, boiling hydrothermal features.
- Snowshoe and ski in a winter wonderland.
- Climb a cinder cone.

**Address**: Lassen Volcanic National Park Headquarters, 38050 Hwy 36 E., Mineral, CA
**Tel.**: (530) 595-4480
**Websites**: www.nps.gov/lavo, www.lassenparkfoundation.org, www.lassenassociation.org

**Best season:**
June to October

! Roads are not plowed in winter

↗ **Lassen's winter is long-lasting, leaving the peak covered with snow even into mid-summer.**

Before the 1980 eruption of Washington's Mount St. Helens, Lassen Peak was the most recently erupted volcano in the contiguous United States. It first blew its top in May 1914, and its volcanic outbursts continued for 7 years. This prominent volcano is the centerpiece of Lassen Volcanic National Park, but it's only one of the park's many fascinating examples of geothermal activity. Scattered among 106,000 acres of deep-green conifer forests and crystal-clear lakes are steaming sulfur vents, mud pots, boiling thermal pools and other out-of-this-world volcanic features.

In winter and spring, Lassen is a popular ski mountaineering and back-country snowboard destination, but even snow-sports novices can strap on a pair of snowshoes and explore the beauty of Lassen cloaked in white. Your car won't be useful at Lassen in February; the park road isn't plowed. But both the north entrance at Manzanita Lake and south entrance (Kohm Yah-mah-nee Visitor Center) have marked snowshoe trails. Bring your own snowshoes and set off on your own, or go for a ranger-guided snowshoe walk, offered most weekends. After the road is plowed in late spring, back-country skiers hike up Lassen Peak's south side, then ski down. The south and west faces offer exciting runs with

↑ **Hot thermal water blows off steam at several park sites, including Terminal Geyser in Warner Valley.**

about 4,000 feet of decent slopes. But you have to earn it — there are no ski lifts here.

Overnight lodging, restaurants and groceries can be found in Mineral or Chester (south side of the park), or in Old Station or Shingletown (north side). Within the park, eight campgrounds offer a range of camping experiences. All of the park's camps are set between 5,600 and 6,700 feet in elevation, so expect warm days and chilly nights.

## Lassen Peak

This now-quiet volcano lies at the very southern end of the Cascade Range, which stretches all the way to British Columbia. As much as 40 feet of snow can fall here in winter, but when it finally melts away in mid-summer, you can hike to Lassen Peak's 10,457-foot summit via a steep 2.5-mile trail. The seemingly barren, silent mountain bears the signs of the eruptions that flattened trees and devastated the landscape for miles around. The peak's eruptions began in May 1914, but the heaviest devastation didn't occur until 1 year later. Steam eruptions continued until 1921.

This is the park's most popular trail, and it's easy enough

↑ **Lassen's mid-summer bloom delivers striking bouquets of salmon-colored Indian paintbrush (top), sweet-scented purple lupine (middle) and sunny yellow mule's ears (bottom).**

for families who've planned properly (start early in the morning to beat the heat, carry plenty of water, and wear sun hats). The path begins on a deceptively mellow grade through a forest of mountain hemlock and whitebark pines, but steepens as it climbs above the trees. A series of switchbacks ascend to Lassen's first summit, where most hikers take in the expansive view and call it a day. To see the peak's crater, you need to continue a short distance farther to a second, slightly higher summit.

With proper timing, your hike might be embellished by a flowery outburst. It seems like nothing would grow where towering gas clouds and massive mudslides once reigned, but instead, Lassen Peak's slopes are covered in silverleaf lupine, its blue-purple blossoms brightening the gray soil. Keep on the lookout for Lassen Peak *smelowskia*, which grows here and nowhere else in the world. Its white tufts peek out from rocky crevices, giving credence to its common name — alpine false candytuft. Also look for pussy paws, its flowers resembling furry cat paws (if cats were pink).

Visitors who would rather drive, not hike, can admire Lassen Peak from Lake Helen, which is nestled at its base. This high-elevation lake often is snow-covered into mid-summer, coloring its waters an icy turquoise. A picnic area to the east is a great spot for lunch.

## Bumpass Hell

The "hell" in Bumpass Hell is aptly named. Bumpass Hell is geology in action — 16 acres of boiling springs, hissing steam vents, noisy fumaroles and bubbling mud pots. Kendall Vanhook Bumpass was the unlucky man who discovered these hydrothermal features in the 1860s — he found them by falling into a boiling pool and burning his leg. A 3-mile round-trip trail travels to the geothermal site. Your nose will tell you when you're getting close.

Although water in the form of steam and carbon dioxide makes up 95 percent of the materials billowing upward from the steam vents,

↑ **Bumpass Hell's hydrothermal basin is a colorful mosaic of turquoise hot pools, mineral-crusted ash and lingering snowfields.**

it's the traces of hydrogen sulfide that leave the biggest impression. The rotten egg smell is pervasive, and so is the noise — a strange ruckus created by all the belching mud pots and bubbling pools. A raised boardwalk trail lets you walk safely around them.

## Sulphur Works

Perched right next to the park road, Sulphur Works is the only geothermal feature in Lassen that is accessible without hiking. It's impossible to miss: steam rises to the sky and clay minerals splash a yellow, orange and red palette across the barren andesite rock. A short interpretive path loops around odoriferous steam vents (you will smell "rotten eggs," or hydrogen sulfide), rumbling fumaroles and bubbling mud pools.

Sulphur Works had a long commercial history — an Austrian businessman started a sulfur mining operation here in 1865, but when demand for sulfur slowed, he switched to tourism. Supan's Springs became the place to go to enjoy a hot mineral bath. It was so popular that by 1941, this site had a gas station,

**↑↗ Right alongside the park road at Sulphur Works, steam rises to the sky, hot pools belch gas and rumbling fumaroles make a joyful noise.**

lunchroom, bathhouse and large restaurant known as The Sulphur Works Inn.

## Manzanita Lake and Loomis Museum

One of the most photographed lakes in Lassen and the centerpiece of the park's northern visitor area, Manzanita Lake offers plenty of recreation options: swimming, kayak rentals, ranger-led programs, cabin rentals, a large campground and camp store, and a 1.6-mile hiking trail that circles the lake. On its north side, photographers find great vantage points for capturing Lassen Peak's monolithic volcanic cone reflecting in the lake's blue water. Visit the Loomis Museum, which features B.F. Loomis' original photographs of Lassen Peak's 1914 eruption, as well as a collection of Native American basketry.

## Waterfall Hikes

Most of Lassen Volcanic National Park's attractions are centered around heat, steam and boiling water, which makes these two family-friendly hikes to cool waterfalls especially refreshing. Pick one or hike both: they're short and easy enough to do in a day. Starting from Southwest Campground at the park's southern entrance, Mill Creek Falls can be reached via a gentle walk that passes through a massive field of mountain mule's ears, their sunflower-like flowers gleaming in the light. The trail leads 1.9 miles to Mill

**↑ During the calm days of autumn, Lassen Peak's cone-shaped profile is reflected in Manzanita Lake.**

**→ The easy hike to Kings Creek Falls is an ideal trek for families and waterfall lovers.**

↑ **The Painted Dunes' colorful palette of ash and pumice entices visitors to northern Lassen's Butte Lake region.**

Creek Falls, the park's highest waterfall at 75 feet tall.

Farther north up the main park road, the Kings Creek Falls hike is only 2.4 miles round-trip. Getting there requires a downhill tromp through a verdant meadow, then a descent on a rocky staircase alongside Kings Creek. The boisterous waterfall is about 50 feet high and tucked into a shady canyon. Arrive in the late morning for your best chance of good photos.

## Painted Dunes and Cinder Cone

A swirling watercolor landscape of orange and gray pumice fields, Lassen's Painted Dunes were formed by the oxidation of volcanic ash from a 700-foot-tall cinder cone. This artist's palette of colorful hills attracts legions of photographers to the Butte Lake region of Lassen Volcanic National Park, an hour's drive from the park's north entrance. Bring plenty of water for the sun-exposed, 4-mile hike.

From Butte Lake Campground, walk a mile through sparse pine forest to Cinder Cone's base. Catch a glimpse of the Painted Dunes from here, then make the thigh-pumping climb up the cone's gravel slope. It's only 2 miles to the top, but this may well be Lassen's most challenging trek. The cinder cone, composed of volcanic ash and gravel, is completely exposed to the sun, and the loose cinders are an exercise in one-step-up, two-steps-back. At the top, the panorama makes it all worthwhile. The otherworldly Painted Dunes steal the show, but Lassen Peak, Prospect Peak and the Fantastic Lava Beds also command attention. Walk the perimeter of Cinder Cone's rim to take in the full 360. Scientists believe this cinder cone erupted only about 350 years ago, not just once, but twice.

**↑ A challenging hike to the top of the otherworldly Cinder Cone offers sweeping views of Lassen Park.**

# Redwood National and State Parks

***A 40-mile stretch of parklands celebrates the coast redwood tree, the world's tallest living thing***

## Hot Spot Highlights

- Wander among ancient redwood trees more than 30 stories high.
- Walk through a stream canyon bounded by towering, fern-covered walls.
- See massive Roosevelt elk grazing in grassy prairies.

**Addresses**: Thomas H. Kuchel Visitor Center, US 101 at Orick, CA; Crescent City Visitor Center, 1111 Second Street, Crescent City, CA
**Tel.**: Thomas H. Kuchel Visitor Center: (707) 465-7765
Crescent City Visitor Center: (707) 465-7335
**Website**: www.nps.gov/redw

**Best season:**
Year-round

**↗ The Pacific coast from Crescent City to Humboldt Bay is a wild, windswept stretch of blue.**

**→ Every redwood hike in these parklands will have you craning your neck at the sky-scraping trees.**

A day spent in California's ancient redwood forests, where the treetops seem to scrape the sky, puts 6-foot-tall humans in their place. With an average lifespan of 500 to 700 years — although many live as long as 2,000 years — coast redwoods can grow to over 370 feet in height, as long as they are protected from the logger's saw. Skirting California's northwestern edge from Crescent City to Orick, a mosaic of jointly managed federal and state parklands contains 45 percent of California's remaining old-growth redwood forest. In the company of these massive trees, Roosevelt elk graze in grassy prairies, and driftwood piles up on windswept beaches.

### Redwood National Park

Start your visit at the Thomas H. Kuchel Visitor Center, 1 mile south of Orick. This is the

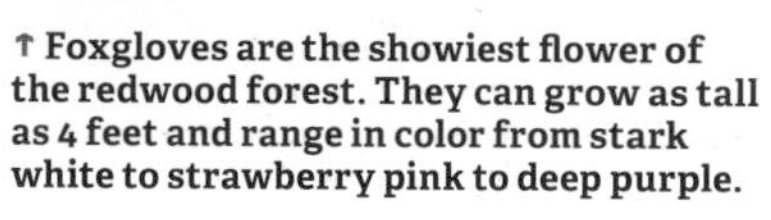

↑ Foxgloves are the showiest flower of the redwood forest. They can grow as tall as 4 feet and range in color from stark white to strawberry pink to deep purple.

↗ Red clintonia thrives in the redwood forest's dense shade. After the flowers are finished, the plant produces blue berries.

→ One big reason these redwoods grow so tall is because the North Coast receives 60 to 80 inches of rain per year.

↑ **Sea stacks, or small rocky islands that remain from the Pleistocene era, are common along the Crescent City coastline.**

largest of five visitor centers in Redwood National and State Parks, with numerous exhibits, a video on redwood ecology, a bookstore and access to a sandy beach. Check with the rangers to see if permits are available for the Tall Trees Grove. If the answer is yes, this should be your first destination. (The Park Service limits the number of cars because of the grove's narrow access road.) The Tall Trees Grove redwoods are not just tall but mind-bogglingly immense, towering as high as 379 feet. A 1.3-mile downhill hike leads to the grove, set on a moist floodplain alongside Redwood Creek. All the trees are behemoths, but the 368-foot Libby Tree commands attention because it was long considered the tallest tree in the world. It lost its status when a 379-footer was found in 2006. The location of the "new" tallest tree has been kept secret, but it's somewhere in this watershed. Several side trails lead from the giant trees to the gravel banks of Redwood Creek.

Several shorter trails are also worth your time. If you're limited by time, walk the easy 1-mile Lady Bird Johnson Grove loop among towering redwood sentinels (the trailhead is 1 mile north of Orick off Bald Hills Road). Near the town of Klamath, the Yurok Loop travels to pristine Hidden Beach (2.2 miles round-trip). In the spring

↑ **Sitka spruce grow in moist, foggy areas along the coast from Alaska south to Northern California.**

↓ **The skunk cabbage has gigantic leaves, but despite its size, you might smell it before you see it. The plant's putrid aroma is designed to lure pollinators.**

months, take a walk on the Skunk Cabbage section of the Coastal Trail. A relative of the corn lily, skunk cabbages grow to huge sizes; their individual leaves can measure a yard long. When flowering, the plant produces a distinctive and rather unpleasant odor, earning its skunky name.

## Prairie Creek Redwoods State Park

In the small town of Orick, this 14,000-acre state park has 75 miles of trails to explore. Start with a hike among ancient redwoods on the 3.2-mile Prairie Creek and Cathedral Tree loop, which begins at Prairie Creek Visitor Center. Moss covers rocks, lichens hang from branches, redwood sorrel carpets the ground, and trees grow to gargantuan size. Next, head over to Elk Prairie, a golden meadow that's a popular hangout spot for 1,000-pound Roosevelt elk. The regal beasts are California's largest land animals and the largest elk species in North America. About 500 elk roam throughout Redwood National and State Parks, and they're often seen alongside roads and near campgrounds — wherever there are grasses to eat. Although they seem docile enough as they languidly chow on meadow grass, it's smart to give them some space. In late summer and fall, the males compete for females by sparring with their seven- and eight-point antlers, which weigh up to 80 pounds.

For visitors who prefer driving over walking, the park's 10-mile Newton B. Drury Scenic Parkway winds past silent groves that reach for the sky. (It's an alternate route to US 101.) Stop along the way to walk 100 yards to the aptly named Big Tree (304 feet tall and 21 feet wide).

A 9-mile drive on Davison Road leads to spectacular Fern Canyon, a hidden paradise of ferns lining a narrow gorge carved out by Home Creek. A scene from *The Lost World: Jurassic Park* was filmed in this verdant canyon, where drooping ferns create hanging gardens, miniature waterfalls pour over rock faces, and moss wallpapers every log and rock. Seven different types of ferns cling to the steep cliffs. Some are ancient species, with ancestry tracing back 325 million years. Underneath their fronds live some special amphibians, including Pacific giant salamanders up to 10 inches long. The Fern Canyon "trail" travels up the stream via a series of small footbridges and stones placed for rock-hopping. (River sandals come in handy during spells of high water.) The canyon walls grow taller and squeeze tighter as you head upstream. In a half mile, the trail curves left and ascends out of the canyon, then loops back to the parking lot.

**↑ A series of bridges line the path into beautiful Fern Canyon, but depending on how high the stream is flowing, you might still get your feet wet.**

**↑↑ Massive Roosevelt elk graze alongside roads and campgrounds on the Redwood Coast at any spot where grass is plentiful.**

## Jedediah Smith Redwoods State Park

East of Crescent City, Jedediah Smith Redwoods State Park sits beside the emerald Smith River in a glade lush with ferns and old-growth trees. Walk the easy 1-mile Stout Grove loop to see the 340-foot-tall Stout Tree and its behemoth brethren, or take a drive on spectacular Howland Hill Road, a 10-mile winding gravel road through old-growth redwoods. The slow-going road offers close encounters with cathedral-like redwoods — giant trees hug the road so tightly, you can reach out and touch them. Stop along the way to hike the Boy Scout Tree Trail to Fern Falls (5.6 miles round-trip). In addition to the magnificent redwoods, you'll see many varieties of ferns, bigleaf maples, vine maples and Douglas firs.

**↑ When a coast redwood topples, its massive root ball is exposed, and we can see how its shallow roots branch out sideways rather than tunnel downward.**

**← It's easy to feel insignificant when you walk among the mammoth sentinels of Stout Grove, which are nourished by the Smith River floodplain.**

# Patrick's Point State Park and Humboldt Lagoons State Park

***Dramatic sea stacks, rocky headlands and brackish lagoons edge the Trinidad coast***

## Hot Spot Highlights

- Admire dozens of rocky sea stacks on and off the coast.
- Beachcomb for agates and semiprecious stones.
- Hike paths that tunnel through alders and Sitka spruce.
- Kayak and fish at four coastal lagoons.

**Addresses**: Patrick's Point State Park, 150 Patrick's Point Drive, Trinidad, CA;
Humboldt Lagoons State Park, 15336 Hwy 101, Trinidad, CA
**Tel.**: (707) 677-3570
**Websites**:
Patrick's Point: www.parks.ca.gov/?page_id=417
Humboldt Lagoons: www.parks.ca.gov/?page_id=416

**Best season:**
Year-round

Thousands of years ago, the land mass of the Trinidad coast was submerged in the Pacific's roiling waters. When the ocean receded, chiseled bluffs towered over the sea and dozens of 100-foot-high outcrops were left standing high and dry. These rock formations, known as "sea stacks," are the signature feature of Patrick's Point State Park and some of the north coast's most photogenic icons.

With a short trek on the park's Rim Trail, you'll visit two landlubbing sea stacks, dubbed Ceremonial Rock and Lookout Rock. Just off the coast, their isolated cousins are continually battered by churning ocean waves. Rim Trail follows the shady route of an old Yurok Indian pathway across the ocean bluffs, tunneling through a forest of Sitka spruce, Douglas fir, red alder and pine. An understory of salmonberry, thimbleberry and ferns covers every inch of ground. In late summer and

fall, the park is thick with berries and bears. Spurring off the main path are short detours leading to high coastal promontories — Wedding Rock, Patrick's Point and Rocky Point. Carved-rock stairs, built by the California Conservation Corps in the 1930s, climb to the top of castle-like Wedding Rock, where you'll find postcard views of Trinidad Head to the south and crashing waves below. In spring and fall, gray whales pass by, and in summer, humpback whales feed close to shore.

On the park's north side, beachcombers descend the set of wooden stairs to 2-mile-long Agate Beach, a white crescent of sand backed by wooded headlands. At low tide, it's possible to find sea-polished agates, moonstones and other bits of semiprecious stones here.

Two miles north of Patrick's Point State Park lies Big Lagoon, the first of several coastal lagoons between Trinidad and Orick that

**↑ From Patrick's Point to Humboldt Lagoons, Trinidad's come-hither beaches invite long strolls and lingering sunset picnics.**

**↖ Lace lichen, sometimes called "old man's beard," hangs from the trees at Patrick's Point. Some birds use it to make soft nests for their eggs.**

← Near Wedding Rock, a trail leads to a rockstrewn beach, where you might find semi-precious agates or jade.

↙ When the sun shines on the Trinidad coast, the Pacific takes on a Caribbean shade of blue.

are managed as Humboldt Lagoons State Park. A few of the lagoons are separated from the ocean by spits of sand, rendering them brackish — part freshwater and part saltwater. The latter rushes in when the sand spits are breached by high-splashing waves during winter storms. This watery three-way intersection of ocean, ponds and marshes is a bonanza for wildlife. Bird sightings are dependably rich. Look for pygmy owls, belted kingfishers, grebes, herons, ospreys and an array of waterfowl.

Stop at the Stone Lagoon Visitor Center along Highway 101 to rent a kayak or stand-up paddleboard from Kayak Zak's and ply the waters. Take a dip in Stone Lagoon's warm(ish) waters, stroll Big Lagoon's driftwood-laden beach or hike along the edge of Dry Lagoon to watch for grazing Roosevelt elk and scampering river otters. (Dry Lagoon was drained by farmers in the 1800s and is now a marsh.) You can even paddle yourself to sleep at Stone Lagoon's boat-in campground, nestled in a grove of Sitka

↑ **Each of the lagoons at Humboldt Lagoons State Park is a watery conglomeration of ocean, pond, beach and marsh.**

→ **A pair of Ross' geese plies the waters at Stone Lagoon.**

spruce, alder and willows.

The lagoons and their adjacent beaches are popular with anglers. From Big Lagoon's long stretch of sandy beach, the usual catch is surf perch. Big Lagoon's waters are rich with largemouth bass and cutthroat trout. Stone Lagoon supports more than a dozen fish species (freshwater, saltwater and anadromous, which live in both kinds of water). Anglers often reel in cutthroat trout (only barbless hooks and artificial lures are permitted).

# Mendocino State Parks

***Pounding surf, rocky outcrops and picturesque headlands frame a string of California state parks***

## Hot Spot Highlights

- Walk through a forest of dwarf pine and cypress trees.
- Lounge in the soft sands of Jug Handle Beach.
- Bicycle to a waterfall hidden in a forested grotto.
- Paddle an outrigger canoe up the Big River.

**Address**: Ford House Visitor Center and Museum, 45035 Main Street, Mendocino, CA
**Tel.**: (707) 937-5397
**Website**: www.mendoparks.org

**Best season:**
Year-round

↗ **Seaside daisies (also known as fleabane or beach asters) cling in dense masses to Mendocino's coastal bluffs.**

In arts-rich Mendocino, perfectly manicured Victorian homes with picket fences and glorious gardens perch on rocky coastal bluffs rising 50 feet above the surf. Founded in the 1850s, Mendocino flourished because of its redwood mill, but when the timber industry declined in the 1930s, artists and craftspeople moved in. Tourism soon followed. The remaining redwoods have been preserved — along with pristine rivers, wildlife-rich wetlands and bucolic coastal headlands — in a string of California state parks.

### Van Damme State Park

Two miles south of Mendocino's artistic hamlet, Van Damme State Park lies in a narrow valley with a protected beach. Its sandy drive-up beach sits at the Little River's mouth and attracts abalone divers, beachcombers and kayakers. Inland, you can hike or bike 3.5 miles on the lush Fern Canyon Trail, which crosses back and forth over Little River beneath second-growth redwoods. Or take a walk on the wheelchair-accessible trail through the park's pygmy forest (3 miles up Little River Airport Road), where acidic

↑ **Thickly vegetated headlands punctuated by tiny dots of islands comprise a classic Mendocino coastal scene.**

soil and a layer of nearly impenetrable hardpan result in fully mature pine and cypress trees reaching only about waist high, even though they might be a century old.

## Big River Unit, Mendocino Headlands State Park

Eight miles long, Big River is the longest undeveloped estuary in California and home to river otters, harbor seals, beavers, fox and more than 130 bird species. The best way to see it is to get out on the water. Bring your own kayak or rent a handcrafted redwood outrigger canoe from Catch a Canoe and paddle away (www.catchacanoe.com). Outrigger canoes are nearly impossible to tip, and you get to sit upright in a real seat. As you travel upriver, you'll find no highways or buildings, just gentle tidal flows, hidden marshes, dense forests and abundant animal life.

## Russian Gulch State Park

Extending from the beach to a shady interior forest, Russian Gulch is an unspoiled slice of coast and canyon just 2 miles north of Mendocino.

The park's coastal side contains craggy bluffs laced with wildflowers, walking trails and a coastal blowhole known as the Devil's Punchbowl — actually a collapsed sea arch frequented by splashing waves. (During big storms, you might get lucky enough to see a saltwater geyser shoot upward through the hole, but most of the year, inbound waves roll gently in and out.)

Heading inland, you'll find Russian Gulch's 36-foot-tall waterfall tucked into a forested grotto. You can see it on a bicycle or on foot. Bicyclists follow the 1.6-mile paved Fern Canyon Trail through a dense riparian forest of second-growth redwoods, hemlocks, Douglas firs, bigleaf maples, alders and a multitude of ferns. In the rainy season, you might spot rainbow and steelhead trout in the creek. Where the pavement ends, lock up your bike and continue on foot on Falls Loop Trail. Hikers can follow the same route or take the undulating North Trail instead — a longer, less-traveled path that roughly parallels Fern Canyon Trail. Either way, you'll soon find yourself at the foot of Russian Gulch Falls, a petite cataract that drops into a verdant, fern-lined grotto. In winter, the waterfall is a rushing torrent spilling over broken tree trunks and branches that have accumulated at its base.

In the drier summer months, it's a more delicate cascade, framed by ferns and moss.

## Jug Handle State Natural Reserve

Midway between Mendocino and Fort Bragg, wander the blufftop trails at Jug Handle State Natural Reserve and you may see gray whales spout as they pass by on their annual migration from Mexico to Alaska. Like most of Mendocino County's coastline, this stretch is punctuated by sea stacks and caves carved out by the pounding surf. In April and May, the bluffs are peppered with golden poppies, Indian paintbrush, coastal lupine, seaside daisies and wild strawberries.

Beachgoers will cherish the park's near-perfect cove of white sand on Jug Handle Bay. The Pacific is often too rough for swimming, but kids can frolic in the shallow flow of Jug Handle Creek while adults watch waves crash, seals dive and pelicans plunge.

For a botany and geology lesson, hike the 5-mile Ecological Staircase Nature Trail that begins near the beach, then heads under the highway bridge and along Jug Handle Creek's streambed. The trail ascends three wave-cut terraces, each 100,000 years older than the last and with distinct flora ranging from coastal prairie to giant redwoods. Marine terraces are common along the California coast, but they are rarely as

**↑ At the end of the Ecological Staircase Nature Trail, the highest marine terrace gives rise to a pygmy forest of stunted pine and cypress trees.**

**↖ On sunny days, Jug Handle's crescent of white sand is a fine place to lay out a towel and read a book.**

**← A 6-foot-tall man seems Lilliputian when standing at the lip of Russian Gulch Falls.**

↑ **Pacific coast native irises range in color from cream to golden yellow to lavender to blue-violet. Local Native Americans used the strong leaf fibers for fish nets and rope.**

↗ **Spring-fed Lake Cleone is a great spot for paddling a kayak or birdwatching.**

well preserved and easily distinguishable as here. These terraces formed during the Pleistocene era as sea levels fluctuated. The geological evolution continues to this day, with future terraces still underwater. The first terrace is a grassland ecosystem dotted with occasional bishop pines. The second is a mixed conifer forest of bishop pine, Douglas fir, redwood and Sitka spruce. (Sitka spruce, which grow along the Pacific coast all the way to Alaska, are at the far southern end of their range here.) As you progress, you'll notice the pines disappearing and the redwoods taking over. About 2 miles in, you'll reach the third terrace, composed of hardpan soil, sand and a pygmy forest of miniaturized pine and cypress, where 2-foot-high trees are more than a century old, stunted by their environment. The soil in this forest is 300 feet higher than at Jug Handle Beach, but it's 300,000 years older. Linger among the bonsai trees and look for the rare and endemic Bolander pine, which grows only in acidic, nutrient-poor soil.

## MacKerricher State Park

A few miles north of Fort Bragg, this park features an 8-mile-long crescent of sandy beach, roaring surf, blowing dunes and craggy headlands. Follow the easy boardwalk trail around spring-fed Lake Cleone, a 30-acre freshwater lake that's a sure bet for

bird sightings. More than 90 species reside in or visit the lake and its marsh, including mallards, egrets, surf scooters, sanderlings and avocets. Walk to Laguna Point, where harbor seals inhabit the rocks offshore, and migrating gray whales pass by from December to April. For a longer excursion, walk or pedal the Coastal Trail, a paved path following an old logging railway that's been undercut by wave action. To the north, the trail passes miles of dark sand beaches before it disappears into the shifting dunes. Heading south, it crosses the Pudding Creek Railroad Trestle and enters the town of Fort Bragg. The trestle, which is an astonishing 527 feet long and 44 feet high, spans beautiful Pudding Creek Beach. It was built in the early 20th century as part of the timber-hauling Ten Mile Railroad.

**↑ Sea lions haul out on the rocks at Laguna Point, and they cuddle up to share body heat.**

**↖ The Pudding Creek Railroad Trestle connects MacKerricher State Park's Coastal Trail with the town of Fort Bragg.**

# Point Arena-Stornetta Public Lands

***Sea cliffs, blow holes, offshore outcrops and coastal wildflowers highlight this new addition to California Coastal National Monument***

## Hot Spot Highlights

- See the "bowling balls" at one of California's most unusual beaches.
- Walk 5 miles of pristine sand backed by tall dunes.
- Climb to the top of the Point Arena Lighthouse.

**Address**: Point Arena Lighthouse, 45000 Lighthouse Road, Point Arena, CA
**Tel.**: (707) 882-2809
**Websites**:
http://pointarenalighthouse.com,
https://pointarenastornetta.org

**Best season:**
Year-round

↗ **The pigeon guillemot, a member of the auk family, is found near rocky shores from Alaska to California.**

Overshadowed by the tourist-luring town of Mendocino to the north, sleepy Point Arena's main point of interest was geographical — it's the mainland's closest point to Hawaii, so the islands' Internet cable connects here. But since 2014, the tiny hamlet has become the gateway to the recently protected Stornetta Public Lands section of California Coastal National Monument. This new federal designation opens up public access to a dramatic stretch of coastline neighboring one of California's tallest lighthouses. Combined with adjacent coastal lands already preserved by the state, Point Arena now boasts nearly 20 miles of coastline available for exploration.

### Stornetta Public Lands and Point Arena Lighthouse

Formerly a cattle ranch, Stornetta's gently sloping,

grass-covered headlands jut to the northwest in a peninsula that has been cut from the shoreline by the Garcia River. At the very tip of the peninsula is the Point Arena Lighthouse, which reaches 115 feet into the sky, surrounded by water on three sides. Stop in at the visitor center to see a collection of maritime photos and exhibits, then climb 145 steps to the top of this historic landmark,

↑ Sea arches, succulent-covered bluffs and wicked waves are some of the treasures of Point Arena-Stornetta Public Lands.

↑↑ South of Point Arena Lighthouse, rocky shoals meet the endlessly pounding Pacific.

← A steep tromp up a narrow circular staircase leads to the top of Point Arena Lighthouse, one of California's tallest lighthouses.

↑ **Black oystercatchers feed on an array of shellfish including mussels, limpets, chitons, crabs and barnacles — but not oysters.**

where you'll soak in eye-popping views of sea stacks, rock arches and crashing waves. The lighthouse was built in 1870 and severely damaged in the 1906 earthquake, but the rebuilt tower's powerful light still shines.

Next, drive Lighthouse Road to the trailhead 1 mile south of the lighthouse. Hike the path that starts here to see blowholes, sea caves, tide pools and lingering sunsets. Wave-battered sea stacks form a dotted line off this jagged coast, and there's even a waterfall in the wet season, when Stornetta Falls cascades 40 feet over the coastal bluffs. If you can't bear to leave this beautiful area, book a stay at the lighthouse in the former Coast Guard homes nearby.

## Manchester State Park

The dunes at Manchester Beach back a driftwood-laden swath of sand, ideal for long walks spent searching for washed-in treasures. You can leave thousands of footprints on this 5-mile-long beach. The dunes are worth exploring too, especially in spring,

when seasonal wildflowers burst into bloom — sea pinks, poppies, lupine and more. Two streams, Brush Creek and Alder Creek, offer steelhead fishing. Northern harriers soar over the dunes, and in winter, tundra swans winter near the wetland lagoons and the Garcia River. Swimming is not recommended, as the surf pounds the beach here.

## Bowling Ball Beach

While in Point Arena, be sure to check your tide table. During very low tides, walk from Schooner Gulch State Beach (3.5 miles south of Point Arena) to Bowling Ball Beach to see its astounding assemblage of round rocks formed by millions of years of weathering. The oddly spherical "balls" are actually concretions — unusually well-cemented aggregates that are found in the sedimentary rocks that make up the cliffs. Over millions of years, the softer surrounding rock has eroded away under the Pacific's constant onslaught, leaving the tougher "bowling balls" behind.

**↑ Point Arena's beaches produce abundant seashells, like this sunset-hued scallop shell.**

**↖ Visit Bowling Ball Beach at a very low or minus tide, and you'll be amazed at the symmetry of these spherical sandstone concretions.**

# Salt Point State Park

***Meandering trails lead across ocean-worn headlands, where sandstone, surly waves and the sundown sea intersect***

## Hot Spot Highlights

- Camp and hike on the Sonoma Coast's dramatic wind-carved headlands.
- Explore tafoni sandstone formations and wildflower-laden bluffs.
- Dive for abalone during the legal fishing season.

**Address**: Salt Point State Park, 25050 Hwy 1, Jenner, CA
**Tel.**: (707) 847-3221
**Websites**: www.parks.ca.gov/?page_id=453, www.saltpoint.org

**Best season:**
Year-round

**↗ Salt Point's bluffs are decorated with *tafoni*, a honeycombed sandstone formation caused by wind and water erosion.**

Salt Point State Park encompasses 6,000 acres of Sonoma County's west coast — a wildly beautiful meeting of sea and land. Wind-lashed headlands are crowned with grassy terraces, and sandstone cliffs drop abruptly to the sea. The waters near the park are protected as Salt Point State Marine Conservation Area, one of California's first underwater parks, filled with kelp beds teeming with sea life.

Bisected by Highway 1, the park offers visitors a bounty of treasures to see and explore from its picnic areas and overlook points — you barely need to get out of your car to enjoy much of its beauty. Follow the park's main road to Gerstle Cove and Salt Point, where bluffs are lined with honeycombed sandstone formations called *tafoni*, an Italian word for "caverns." Swiss-cheese-like holes in the rock are caused by wind and water erosion. Wind-whipped waves continually lash the shore, depositing a fascinating variety of stones and shells.

Hikers can choose from 20 miles of trails: the 1.2-mile Salt Point Trail traces along the headlands to Stump Beach Cove, one of the few sandy beaches on this stretch of coast. A steep 1-mile hike from Woodside Campground leads through stands of Douglas firs and bishop pines to a pygmy forest of stunted cypress and pine trees. Or, drive north from the main park entrance to Fisk Mill Cove, where you might see wetsuit-clad divers plunging into the ocean to extract the gastronomist's favorite gastropod. Abalone hunting off the California coast has been strictly regulated since the 1990s, but nonetheless, the state's abalone population is sadly in decline. (In 2018, the abalone season was cancelled altogether.)

At Fisk Mill Cove, take a walk on the easygoing Bluff Trail. The nearly level path meanders through a forest of ferns, rhododendrons, cypress, and bishop pines, providing peekaboo views of rocky pocket beaches with crashing waves and playful seals swimming in the surf. In the spring, a few tiny meadows are carpeted with purple Douglas irises. Near the trail's end, climb to the top of Sentinel Rock, a dramatic coastal overlook. A bench on top invites you to stay awhile, but allow time for a short side-trip to rocky Fisk Mill Cove. You might find some interesting stones for your rock collection.

Salt Point State Park has two campgrounds that lie on opposite sides of the road, offering sites suitable for variable weather. Gerstle Cove Campground provides ocean views for calm days, and pine-shaded Woodside Campground shelters campers from the frequent coastal wind.

↑ California's state colors — blue and gold — are echoed in this coastal blufftop garden of lupine and California poppies.

↑↑ Sentinel Rock's vista takes in the cobbled shoreline of Fisk Mill Cove, a popular rock-hounding site.

↖ Observant petal-peepers may spot earth brodiaea, a tiny purple bulb flower that blooms on Salt Point's blufftop grasslands.

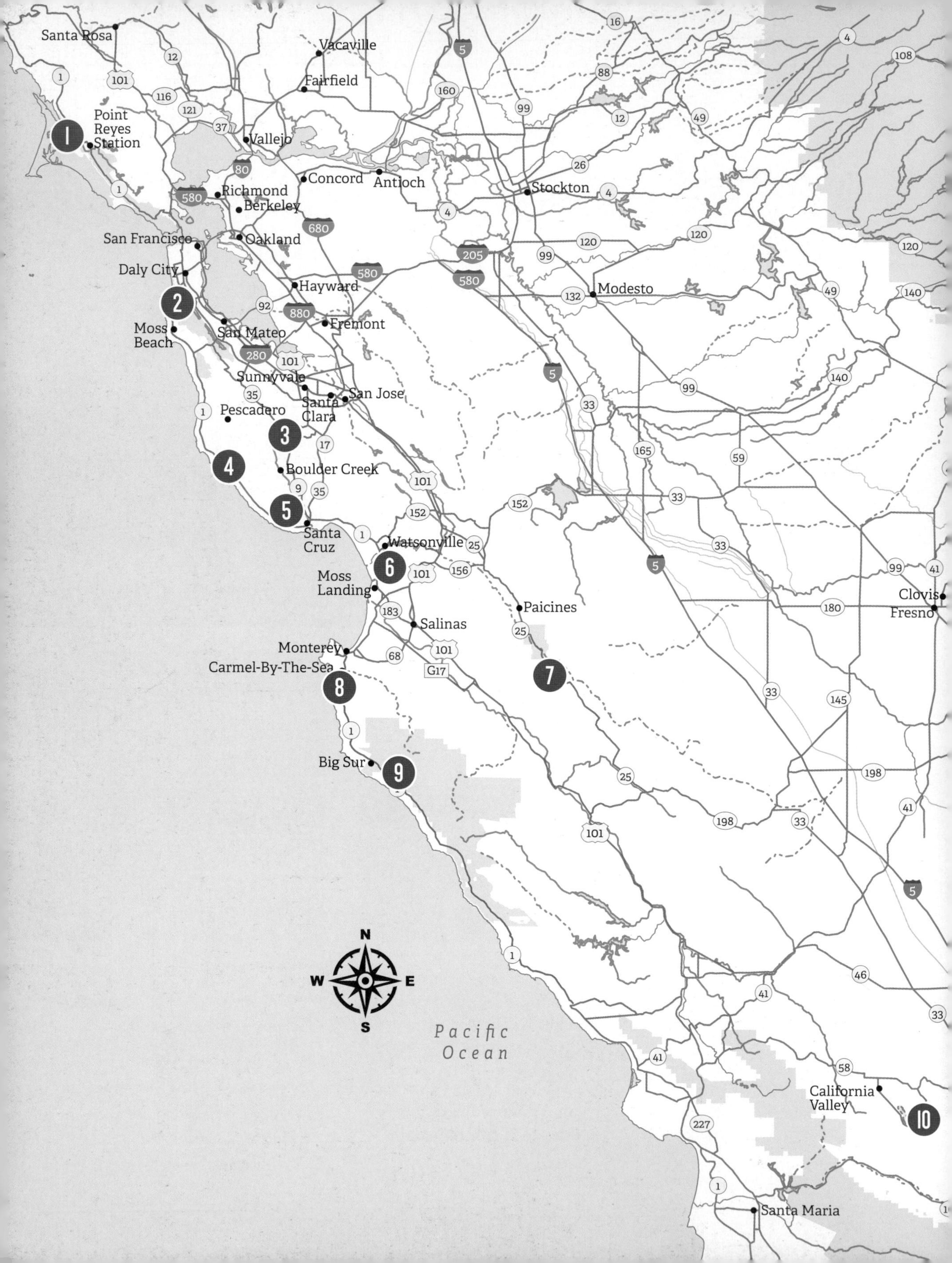

Santa Rosa
Vacaville
Fairfield
Point Reyes Station
Vallejo
Concord
Antioch
Richmond
Berkeley
Stockton
San Francisco
Oakland
Daly City
Hayward
Modesto
Moss Beach
San Mateo
Fremont
Sunnyvale
San Jose
Santa Clara
Pescadero
Boulder Creek
Santa Cruz
Watsonville
Moss Landing
Salinas
Paicines
Clovis
Fresno
Monterey
Carmel-By-The-Sea
Big Sur
Pacific Ocean
California Valley
Santa Maria
N
W
E
S
1
2
3
4
5
6
7
8
9
10

# San Francisco Bay Area and Central Coast

# Point Reyes National Seashore

***A fog-kissed peninsula that protects more than 1,500 animal and plant species***

## Hot Spot Highlights

- Witness a dramatic meeting of land and sea.
- See tule elk, elephant seals and gray whales.
- Walk along miles of deserted beaches.
- Visit the iconic Point Reyes Lighthouse.

**Address**: Bear Valley Visitor Center, 1 Bear Valley Visitor Center Access Road, Point Reyes Station, CA
**Tel.**: (415) 464-5100
**Websites**: www.nps.gov/pore, www.ptreyes.org

**Best season:**
Year-round

**↗ California has two elk species — the massive Roosevelt elk and smaller tule elk. Here, tule elk bulls gather near Point Reyes' Tomales Point for their autumn rut, when they compete for females.**

Jutting dramatically into the blue Pacific, the West Coast's only national seashore extends across 70,000 acres of a large triangular peninsula that appears to have broken away from the Northern California coast. The coastal preserve, an hour north of San Francisco, protects more than 1,500 animal and plant species in a watery utopia of beaches, lagoons, estuaries and ponds that surround a densely wooded interior. Here, breakers pound remote beaches, wisps of fog wash over coastal hills, elephant seals brawl on the sand and tule elk roam in wild meadows.

In this lush green-and-blue wonderland, binoculars and hiking boots are required equipment. Dress in layers for variable weather (fog and wind are common year-round). Stop in at the park's Bear Valley Visitor Center to get updates on whale watching (January to mid-April), wildflower displays (best in May), elk viewing, and hiking trail conditions. Smaller visitor centers are located at Drakes Beach and the Point Reyes Lighthouse.

With more than 80 miles of Pacific shoreline, the Point

↑ **A carpet of tidy tips graces the Pacific side of Arch Rock.**

Reyes peninsula provides an array of seaside options for strolling, sunbathing, kayaking, kite flying and birdwatching. If you want to drive right up and plop down in the sand, head to Drakes Beach. Backed by tall cliffs, this sheltered cove provides refuge from Point Reyes' blustery winds and safe swimming in the relatively calm waters of Drakes Bay. Look for the small memorial to Sir Francis Drake, who may have harbored his ship the *Golden Hinde* here in 1579 while exploring the New World. A small visitor center and bookstore are open on weekends. Nearby is Point Reyes Beach, also known as the Great Beach or Ten-Mile Beach, which spans across 11 captivating miles of sand and surf. You never know what you'll see on a long walk here, but count on brayed-tan sand, wild waves and unforgettable sunsets. (Walk from the parking lots at North Beach or South Beach.) You can also drive to Limantour Beach, located about 20 minutes from Bear Valley Visitor Center. The mile-long beach is backed by low, grassy dunes, so it's ideal for picnicking, even on windy days.

← On the northern tip of the Point Reyes peninsula, fiddlenecks bloom in profusion on the bluffs above Kehoe Beach.

↙ A lone deer wanders the marshy grasslands near Abbotts Lagoon.

There's plenty of space for a crowd, including Rover and Lassie — dogs are permitted on the beach's southeast end.

Visitors willing to walk, not drive, can find seclusion at Point Reyes' hike-in beaches, including dog-friendly Kehoe Beach on the peninsula's northern tip. A nearly level trail skirts alongside Kehoe Marsh, where songbirds flit and pink and yellow mustard grows waist-high in the spring. Near the ocean, the marshy terrain morphs into giant sand dunes and sandstone cliffs. Farther north, near Pierce Point Ranch, lies photogenic McClures Beach, set in a cove bookended by rugged cliffs. During low tides, head south to explore rocky tide pools teeming with sea life. At minus tides, a narrow passageway is revealed. Pass through this rock-lined gap to gain access to a secluded cove connected to McClures by a narrow shelf of rock.

Point Reyes has four hike-in campgrounds for backpackers; advance reservations are required. The closest drive-in campground is at Samuel P. Taylor State Park, 10 miles east.

## Tomales Point

Make the drive to Tomales Point to see the tule elk, especially during the fall rutting season. Majestic tule elk — a subspecies found only in California — roam throughout the peninsula, but are especially easy to see near Pierce Point Ranch and on the neighboring Tomales Point Trail. The 500-pound elk were once common, but by the 1870s, they were nearly hunted out of existence. Today Point Reyes' re-established herd consists of more than 500 animals. In late summer, the bull elks are in their rut, and you may hear the males bugling or see them sparring with a raucous clash of 40-pound antlers.

## Abbotts Lagoon

Birdwatchers should head for the brackish waters of Abbotts Lagoon and its neighboring freshwater ponds. More than 45 percent of North America's bird species have been spotted at Point Reyes, and this 200-acre lagoon is a prime location. Follow the trail along its edge to see western grebes, pied-billed grebes, coots, black-shouldered kites and Caspian terns. The autumn migration season is the best time to build up your birder's life list, but you'll find intriguing sightings here year-round.

## Chimney Rock and Point Reyes Lighthouse

In the winter months, more than 1,000 elephant seals take over the beaches and

**← More than 1,000 elephant seals take over the beaches at Chimney Rock from December to April.**

**↙ Western grebes — also called swan-necked grebes because of their gracefully curved necks — visit Abbotts Lagoon in the winter months.**

**→ Point Reyes is a dream-come-true for wildflower fans. Clockwise from top left: yellow goldfields and cream cups, deep purple bog lupine, furry-looking pussy ears, coast Indian paintbrush and lavender Douglas iris.**

give birth to pups at Chimney Rock. Easily identified by their massive size — male elephant seals can grow longer than 18 feet and weigh more than 2 tons — the seals recline on the beaches, battle with their neighbors, flop sand onto their backs with their flippers, and scooch across the sand. To see them, park at the Chimney Rock Trailhead, then walk down the paved road to the Elephant Seal Overlook. By late spring, the show is mostly over, although smaller numbers of seals can be seen in almost every month of the year.

From late April to mid-June, Point Reyes National Seashore attracts droves of flower lovers to its rugged coastal bluffs and mossy Douglas fir forests. The park's champion flower walk is Chimney Rock Trail. In a mere 1.4 miles, you'll find an overflowing banquet of blossoms dotting the blufftop grasslands — poppies, owl's clover, tidy tips, lupine, checkerbloom, mule's ears, paintbrush, Douglas

↑ **Resembling a penguin, the common murre spends the winter at sea, then returns to the coast to nest on steep cliffs and rocky ledges.**

↗ **Three hundred and eight stairsteps descend the bluffs to the Point Reyes Lighthouse, which is perched on the windiest point on the West Coast.**

iris and footsteps-of-spring. Near the trail's end, look for low-growing pussy ears — they're lavender to white with fuzzy hairs on their petals. This short hike provides alluring blue-water views from Chimney Rock's dramatic promontory high above the sea, plus a chance to see elephant seals hauled out on the beaches below.

Perched on the windiest and foggiest point on the West Coast, the Point Reyes Lighthouse no longer operates — it's been replaced by an automated light on the cliffs below — but it's a fine place to gaze wistfully out to sea. A short uphill walk leads to the Lighthouse Visitor Center and an observation deck where you can survey jagged rock outcrops dotted with hundreds of seabirds, including a massive colony of common murres. From here, an impressive 308-step concrete staircase descends to the lighthouse. The Pacific's gleaming surface spreads to the horizon; a tumultuous sea roils below. The breeze rarely ceases here. Forty-mile-per-hour winds are common, so be sure to dress appropriately.

Winter is the prime time for whale watching at Point Reyes. The lighthouse and Chimney Rock are hot spots for sightings, but you may glimpse a

fluke or a dorsal hump from almost any high spot along the coast. Naturalists estimate that between December and February, 94 percent of the gray whale population that feeds in the Bering Sea during the summer — about 30,000 whales — will pass within 1 mile of Point Reyes on the way to Baja, Mexico, to breed and give birth. January is the most whale-happy month, when as many as 2,000 gray whales pass by the peninsula each day. Days with calmer winds are best — the whales' telltale spouts are easiest to spot when the sea has no whitecaps. Volunteers at the lighthouse visitor center keep a daily "whale count" posted on a whiteboard. The number is usually in the hundreds.

On weekends and holidays from January to mid-April, the Park Service operates a mandatory shuttle bus from the Kenneth C. Patrick Visitor Center at Drakes Beach to the lighthouse and Chimney Rock.

**↑ An easy walk on the Chimney Rock Trail provides an opportunity to see myriad spring wildflowers and occasionally passing gray whales.**

**↖ The narrow backbone of the Point Reyes peninsula is hugged by Drakes Bay on the right and the rocky-edged Pacific on the left.**

# Fitzgerald Marine Reserve

***One of the best tide pool regions in Northern California***

### Hot Spot Highlights

- Explore tide pools at one of California's largest intertidal reefs.
- Walk a blufftop trail through windswept cypress trees.
- Stroll the white sands of Seal Cove.

**Address**: Fitzgerald Marine Reserve, 200 Nevada Street, Moss Beach, CA
**Tel.**: (650) 728-3584
**Website**: https://parks.smcgov.org/fitzgerald-marine-reserve

**Best season:**
Winter and spring for the lowest daytime tides (check a tide table)

↗ **A walking path skirts the bluffs above Fitzgerald Marine Reserve, offering a birds-eye view of the intertidal reef.**

→ **Sea anemones spend their time attached to rocks at the intertidal zone, waiting for a fish to pass close enough to get caught by their venom-filled tentacles.**

Pay a visit to Fitzgerald Marine Reserve and you might walk a few miles or only a few yards. But no matter how great or small the distance, it's going to be the slowest walk of your life.

Fitzgerald Marine Reserve is part of the Monterey Bay National Marine Sanctuary, the largest marine sanctuary in the United States, which runs along the coast from Marin County to San Simeon. Within this sanctuary lies a broad, rocky, intertidal reef extending from Point Montara to Pillar Point. It's one of the largest intertidal reefs in California; during the lowest tides, as many as 30 acres of intertidal pools are exposed.

At minus tides, you'll walk at a snail's pace along the reef, moving inch by inch with your head down, staring at the miraculous world lying at your feet. Colorful sea creatures are revealed by the departing sea, and tiny fish scurry along the bottoms of clear, shallow pools. Check the crevices in the rocks and you might see mussels, crabs, abalones, barnacles, starfish, anemones, snails and limpets. If you're lucky, you may spot an octopus or a nudibranch. More than 200 species of marine animals and 150 species of plants can be observed here. Even novice

↑ This pink sea star is a relative of the more common ochre sea star, which may be purple, orange or reddish-brown.

↑↑ Purple sea urchins are a gastronomic delicacy known as uni, but they can't be taken at Fitzgerald Marine Reserve, where all creatures are protected.

↑ **These two bat stars — easily identified by their stubby arms — are common denizens of the low intertidal zone, which is under water 90 percent of the time.**

beachcombers will be richly rewarded — it's virtually impossible not to stare down a starfish or ogle an urchin.

From the parking lot, a wide trail parallels an ocean-bound creek down to the rocky beach. Head to your left toward Pillar Point in Half Moon Bay, 2.5 miles distant. When the tide is out, you could conceivably cover this distance — if you don't get too distracted in the first few hundred feet.

As you walk, watch for the four central zones of a tide pool area. The first is the low intertidal zone, which is under water 90 percent of the time, so you get to see its inhabitants only during the lowest tides of the year. This is where the most interesting creatures are: eels, octopuses, sea hares, brittle stars, giant keyhole limpets, sculpins and bat stars. The second area is the middle intertidal zone, which is under water only 50 percent of the time, so it's in between the low and high tide line. This area has the creatures we usually associate with tide pools: sea stars or starfish, purple sea urchins, sea anemones, gooseneck barnacles, red algae and mussels. In the high intertidal zone (under water only 10 percent of the time), you may find acorn barnacles, shore crabs, black tegulas and hermit crabs. These creatures can live out of water for long periods of time. The final tide pool region is the splash zone, where you find rough limpets, snails and periwinkles.

To see what this reef looks like from above, combine your tide pool exploration with a walk on the blufftop path above the marine reserve. Access the trail via the footbridge near the tide pool parking lot. The path climbs uphill through a hauntingly beautiful cypress forest. Openings between the trees provide breathtaking ocean views. A

↑ **A ghostly forest of cypress trees, bent by the ocean breeze, crown the bluffs above the marine reserve.**

set of stairs leads down to the white-sand beach at Seal Cove.

To optimize your visit, check a tide chart to plan your visit during a low tide or, even better, during a minus tide. During fall and winter when tides are extremely low, rangers offer free nighttime tide pool tours. Armed with a flashlight, you can observe nighttime activity on the reefs.

At any time, be extremely careful as you explore the fragile tide pools. Feel free to look at and even touch the treasures that you find, but don't pick them up or move them. Every rock, plant, shell and marine animal in this marine reserve is protected by federal law.

Plentiful lodgings, restaurants and groceries are available in Half Moon Bay. From the reserve, drive or walk north for a few blocks to the Moss Beach Distillery, where you can dine by the fire pits on the outdoor deck.

# Big Basin Redwoods State Park

***The first parkland in the world designated to protect the magnificent coastal redwood tree***

### Hot Spot Highlights

- See ancient redwoods in California's oldest state park.
- Hike to three glistening waterfalls.
- Birdwatch at Rancho del Oso marsh.

**Address**: Big Basin Redwoods State Park Headquarters and Visitor Center, 21600 Big Basin Way, Boulder Creek, CA
**Tel.**: (831) 338-8860
**Website**: www.parks.ca.gov/bigbasin

**Best season:**
December to June

Featuring an incredible diversity of terrain — from the wind-ruffled Pacific Ocean to the densely forested slopes of the Santa Cruz Mountains — Big Basin Redwoods State Park is one of California's most beloved treasures. It boasts 2,000-year-old redwood trees (the largest continuous stand of old-growth south of San Francisco), a trio of breathtaking waterfalls, 80 miles of well-built trails and a wildlife-rich marsh where the mouth of Waddell Creek meets the sea. Established in 1902, this was California's very first state park.

For an easy introduction, follow the Redwood Loop Trail from park headquarters through a primeval forest. The half-mile trail interprets the unique qualities of the coast redwood — many of these giants are more than 50 feet around and as tall as the Statue of Liberty.

Serious hikers should lace up their boots for a 10-mile trek through ancient old-growth and recovering second-growth redwoods to three comely waterfalls: Berry Creek, Silver and Golden. The Skyline-to-the-Sea Trail meanders among virgin trees, some larger than 12 feet in diameter. The path skirts the edge of a series of creeks: Opal, Kelly and then West Waddell. Watch carefully to avoid stepping on huge yellow banana slugs that crawl across the trail and, in the wet season, California newts that always seem to be underfoot. At 4.2 miles, Skyline-to-the-Sea Trail meets up with Berry Creek Falls Trail. A wooden overlook platform grants you audience with this 65-foot-tall cataract, its flow tumbling over a fern-lined cliff framed by redwoods.

Many hikers are satisfied

with a picnic lunch at this idyllic spot, but two more waterfalls await in the next mile. Above Berry Creek Falls lies Silver Falls, a more delicate cascade that spills over golden-tinted sandstone and limestone. Stairs ascend to its mossy brink and beyond to the lower tumble of Golden Falls Cascade, a multitiered drop formed by orange-tinted sandstone. Turn around here for a 10.4-mile out-and-back trip, or continue onward to make a 12-mile loop via Sunset Trail.

Backpackers can explore more of the park by spending the night at one of several trail camps. A popular overnight trip is to follow Skyline-to-the-Sea Trail all the way to its end at the Pacific Ocean. Near the beach lies the freshwater marsh and the Theodore J. Hoover Natural Preserve. This separate unit of Big Basin, known as Rancho del Oso, is a great destination for birders.

Big Basin is heavily visited, especially on weekends, so time your trip for a weekday if possible.

**↑ At the base of coastal redwoods, you'll find ferns and sorrel covering almost every inch of ground.**

**↖ In Big Basin's dense and dark redwood forest, Berry Creek Falls appears like a shimmering revelation.**

**← The banana slug travels across the forest floor at the tediously slow rate of 6.5 inches per minute.**

# Año Nuevo State Reserve

***A critical breeding location for northern elephant seals***

## Hot Spot Highlights

- Watch thousands of elephant seals socialize and rear their pups.
- Witness the comeback of an endangered species.
- See other pinnipeds, like sea lions and harbor seals.

**Address**: Año Nuevo State Reserve, New Years Creek Road, Pescadero, CA
**Tel.**: (650) 879-2025 or (650) 879-0227
**Website**: www.parks.ca.gov/?page_id=523

**Day use only**

**Best season:**
December 15 to March 31 for largest numbers of elephant seals

**↗ The protruding snout of the male elephant seal allows him to sound his raucous roars and scare off competing males.**

Every winter, tiny Año Nuevo Island and its neighboring beaches play host to one of California's wildest wildlife spectacles. From December through March, this windswept stretch of Pacific coastline is transformed into the breeding grounds of a seething mass of more than 3,000 blubbery northern elephant seals.

The elephant seals' presence here is a remarkable testament to both conservation efforts and nature's ability to recover. By the year 1900, fewer than 100 northern elephant seals were left in the world; the rest had been killed for their blubber. Today the northern elephant seal population has rebounded to approximately 150,000.

These creatures are huge — and not especially cute, like most other seals and sea lions. Their bulky size makes them ungainly. Although they are graceful swimmers, they travel across the sand with gawky, jerking movements. The bull elephant seal's most elephantine characteristic is his bizarre snout, which resembles a short version of an elephant's trunk. He uses it mostly for vocalization, to amplify his strange roars and scare away competitors. The males stage brutal battles with each other as they attempt to collect females for their harems. Even after the breeding period ends, the squabbling continues.

Witness this fantastic show by hiking the reserve's 3-mile Año Nuevo Point Trail. During the peak period (December 15 to March 31), you must reserve tickets in advance for a guided walk with a docent or ranger (www.reservecalifornia.com). Unreserved tickets are sold daily at the park on a first-come, first-served basis, but it's

unwise to drive all the way to the park without reservations. Tickets are the hardest to come by in January, when the baby elephant seals are born.

The trail to reach the elephant seals is a pleasant walk over densely vegetated coastal bluffs and along the edge of a small pond. Beyond the pond, the trail continues west toward Año Nuevo Point, where the elephant seal multitudes come into view. As you near the point, you'll hear a tremendous cacophony of barking and snorting. From this vantage point — typically about 30 feet away — you're close enough to watch the blow-by-blow of the seals' brawls.

Even if you miss the elephant seal breeding season, you can still visit Año Nuevo at almost any time of the year to see pinnipeds. From April to November, you may hike on your own, but you must obtain a free permit at the visitor center or entrance station. Some elephant seals, usually the younger males, will hang around long after the others have departed. The beaches are also popular year-round with California sea lions and harbor seals. From mid-May until mid-August, Steller sea lions breed on an isolated reef surrounding the island.

↑ **Elephant seals seem to have perfected the art of lying around on the beach.**

# Natural Bridges State Beach

***In winter, monarch butterflies upstage a craggy coastline and breathtaking sea arch***

### Hot Spot Highlights

- See boisterous waves crash against a sandstone arch formation.
- Witness thousands of monarch butterflies wintering in a eucalyptus grove.
- Explore tide pools at low tide.

**Address**: 2531 West Cliff Drive, Santa Cruz, CA
**Tel.**: (831) 423-4609
**Website**: www.parks.ca.gov/?page_id=541

**Day use only**

**Best season:**
Mid-October to early February for butterflies

**↗ Every autumn, thousands of monarch butterflies arrive to huddle together in the protected eucalyptus grove at Natural Bridges. By February, they depart, continuing their 2,500-mile journey.**

Thundering waves, an offshore sea arch, and unforgettable sunsets are expected sights at Natural Bridges State Beach, and they're reason enough to visit. But in winter, a nondescript grove of eucalyptus trees near the brayed-tan beach is the temporary home for thousands of migrating butterflies, and these beauties steal the show. Every year from mid-October through early February, the orange-and-black winged insects show up in huge numbers to rest, feed, socialize and mate. In typical years, between 5,000 and 10,000 butterflies winter here.

The only butterflies known to make an annual round-trip migration, monarchs travel from as far north as northern Canada to wintering grounds on either the Pacific coast or the mountains of Michoacán in central Mexico. They tend to choose the same sites year after year, but no single butterfly makes the entire round-trip (it takes several generations to complete the migration). A single monarch's great-grandchildren will eventually make their way back to the same wintering spot that their ancestors preferred — without ever having been there.

To see these remarkable insects at Natural Bridges, walk the 0.25-mile wheelchair-accessible trail to the grove's observation deck.

Warm, sunny days are the best times to see the butterflies in action, flitting in and out of the trees to search for nectar. Eucalyptus trees' winter flowers are an excellent food source. When the temperature drops below 60 degrees Fahrenheit, the butterflies don't fly, but rather huddle together in large masses in the tree branches to conserve their body heat. When they are huddled, you must look closely to see them — they look like big clusters of dead leaves.

Even if you miss the butterfly season, you'll enjoy seeing this park's namesake natural bridge, a spectacular sandstone formation that curves a photogenic arc over the ocean. In the winter months, the bridge is often covered with perching brown pelicans, which can be viewed up close from the overlook area by the entrance kiosk. The beach once had two sandstone bridges, but the second one collapsed in 1980 under assault from a winter storm.

The north side of the park's sandy beach is lined with tide pools, inviting exploration at low tide. Red or ochre sea stars, turban snails, limpets and hermit crabs are some of the denizens that you can spot at low or minus tides. This reef area is considered so ecologically valuable that it was named a State Marine Reserve.

**↑ Non-native ice plant is ubiquitous along the California coast, its colorful flowers blooming almost year-round.**

**↖ Natural Bridges State Beach once had two sandstone arches, but the forces of nature have taken their toll and only one remains.**

# Moss Landing and Elkhorn Slough

***Estuaries, bays, tidal marshes and the deep waters of Monterey Bay attract sea otters, whales and thousands of birds***

## Hot Spot Highlights

- See rafts of sea otters floating near the shore.
- Witness the spectacle of migrating whales.
- Watch shorebirds scurry along the mudflats, and see elegant terns soar overhead.
- Kayak along the waterways of Elkhorn Slough.

**Addresses**: Moss Landing Harbor, 7881 Sandholdt Road, Moss Landing, CA; Elkhorn Slough National Estuarine Research Reserve, 1700 Elkhorn Road, Watsonville, CA
**Tel.**: (831) 728-2822
**Websites**: www.mosslandingharbor.dst.ca.us/IntheArea/outdoorRecreation.htm, www.elkhornslough.org,

**Day use only**

**Best season:**
Year-round

About 30 miles south of Santa Cruz, Highway 1 skirts the Monterey Bay hamlet of Moss Landing, a busy fishing harbor surrounded by a passel of homespun art galleries, roadside antique shops, and slapping-fresh seafood restaurants. Across the highway, a massive steam power plant towers over the waterways and estuaries of Elkhorn Slough, the largest tract of tidal salt marsh outside of San Francisco. This oddly contrasting landscape is the most reliable spot in California to observe sea otters feeding, sleeping, frolicking and caring for their young.

Walk around Moss Landing Harbor and you may see the adorable, furry creatures popping up between the fishing boats. Park your car in the main lot at Moss Landing State Beach (off Jetty Road), walk a few steps toward its protected cove, and you might easily spot dozens of them, particularly groups of bachelor otters huddled together in "rafts." A raft may contain up to 100 otters sleeping side by side, wrapped up in kelp strands so they don't

↑ **Sea otters are highly social creatures, often hanging out together in "rafts" of up to 100 individuals.**

→ **The black-crowned night heron usually hunts in the evening and at night to avoid competing with other birds.**

← **Moss Landing is one of the best places in California to take a whale watching cruise.**

drift too far from each other.

As of 2018, about 3,200 sea otters live near the California coast, and the stretch of Monterey Bay near Moss Landing hosts a large chunk of that population. Sea otters were hunted for their luxurious fur almost to the point of extinction in the 18th and 19th centuries. Their soft, fine coats — the densest fur in the animal kingdom — have about 500,000 hairs per square inch, insulating them from cold water. By the 1930s, less than 100 otters remained in California, but after gaining

↑ **Huge flocks of elegant terns show up at their breeding rookery in Elkhorn Slough in September and October.**

→ **The great egret's long, S-curved neck allows this statuesque shorebird to snatch up fish and frogs as it wades through shallow water.**

protection from the 1973 Endangered Species Act, the animals have staged a remarkable comeback. Scientists are hoping to see their current numbers double in the next decade, but a lot depends on the overall health of the ocean ecosystem. Otters are big eaters — a 60-pound adult consumes at least 15 pounds of food daily, mostly shellfish. That's 25 percent of its body weight, comparable to a human eating roughly 150 quarter-pound hamburgers.

The cuddly otters attract the most attention at Moss Landing, but there's plenty more wildlife to watch. Several Moss Landing tour boats offer half-day and full-day trips to see gray whales and orcas in winter and spring, and humpbacks and blue whales in summer. Seeing a whale is the thrill of a lifetime — its massive, white-barnacled head may shoot out of the ocean to suck air, its tail may slap the water with a resounding crash, or a spray of fire-hose force may blast skyward from its blowhole. A variety of dolphins — Risso's, Pacific white-sided, common and bottlenose — are also present year-round, as well as harbor and Dall's porpoises.

You can witness this spectacle not only from a large boat, but also from the seat of a tiny one-person kayak. Weather permitting, two

companies — Kayak Connection and Venture Quest Kayaking — lead paddlers out of Moss Landing Harbor and into the open ocean to seek out gray whales and humpbacks.

A few miles inland from Moss Landing Harbor, Elkhorn Slough National Estuarine Research Reserve is considered one of the top 100 places in the United States to see birds. The reserve's meandering river channels and wetlands are packed with a huge variety of shorebirds and waterfowl, plus sun-loving harbor seals, sea lions and sea otters. More than 340 bird species reside in or migrate through Elkhorn Slough, including endangered and threatened species such as the brown pelican, California clapper rail, peregrine falcon and California least tern. During the peak of the autumn migration (typically September and October), more than 20,000 birds per day congregate here. The reserve has 5 miles of trails that pass by tidal mudflats, salt marshes and an old dairy barn where owls raise their young. Free, docent-led walks are offered year-round on weekends. Like Moss Landing, you can observe the slough's wildlife at eye level in a kayak. Even beginners can quickly master the basics necessary to propel themselves around the slough's relatively calm waters.

# Pinnacles National Park

***Home to cliffs, crags, and cave structures formed by ancient volcanic eruptions***

## Hot Spot Highlights

- Explore inside dark talus caves.
- Hike through a maze of volcanic cliffs and spires surrounded by wildflowers.
- Rock climb on the pinnacles.
- Scan the skies for endangered California condors.

**Address**: Pinnacles National Park, 5000 Hwy 146, Paicines, CA
**Tel.**: (831) 389-4486
**Websites**: www.nps.gov/pinn, www.pinnacles.org

**Best season:**
March to early May for wildflowers and cooler temperatures

**↗ Trail builders in the 1930s went to great lengths to make the extensive series of paths, tunnels and staircases that meander through Pinnacles National Park.**

The volcano that shaped the landscape of Pinnacles National Park erupted 23 million years ago, 200 miles to the southeast. Shaking and quaking action along the San Andreas Fault carried the volcano's rocks to their present home in the Salinas Valley. The result? A playground of burnished gold boulders and spires where hikers, rock climbers, birdwatchers and cave explorers have plenty of room to roam. Eighty percent of the park is wilderness that can only be explored on foot.

Pinnacles' spires and boulders are a major attraction for rock climbers. If you've climbed elsewhere, keep in mind that this rock is not solid granite. It's much weaker volcanic breccia, and it "gives" a bit easier than granite. The park's east side has somewhat harder, less crumbly rock and more routes that can be top-roped. The beginner climbs "Tourist Trap" and "Discovery Wall" are found to the east, a few minutes' walk from Bear Gulch. The park's west side offers more multipitch routes that require lead climbing. The climbing season runs most of the year, but some

routes are closed from January to July to protect nesting peregrine falcons and eagles.

Thanks to its rich volcanic soil and vast grasslands, Pinnacles is an ideal spot for annual wildflowers. California poppies and purple owl's clover line the creekbeds, mariposa lilies glow bright white in the tall grass, and pink shooting stars cluster near moist springs. More than 80 percent of the park's plants flower between March and May, but in many years you'll find blooms as early as January or February.

Pinnacles National Park is a hiker's paradise in the daytime, but it's even more intriguing at night. The region's dark skies, far from city lights, ensure great stargazing. On most Saturday nights, park rangers lead a 1-hour, 1-mile hike under the stars.

Although it's only a 1.5-hour drive from San Jose, the region surrounding Pinnacles National Park is surprisingly remote, so be sure to plan ahead for lodging and camping, and pack meticulously. The park's one campground is located on its east side (Bear Gulch). The west side is open only from 7:30 a.m. to 8 p.m. daily. Motels

**↑ The High Peaks Trail winds in, over and around rounded formations of volcanic breccia.**

**↓ Pinnacles' extensive grasslands give rise to a spectacular wildflower display in early spring.**

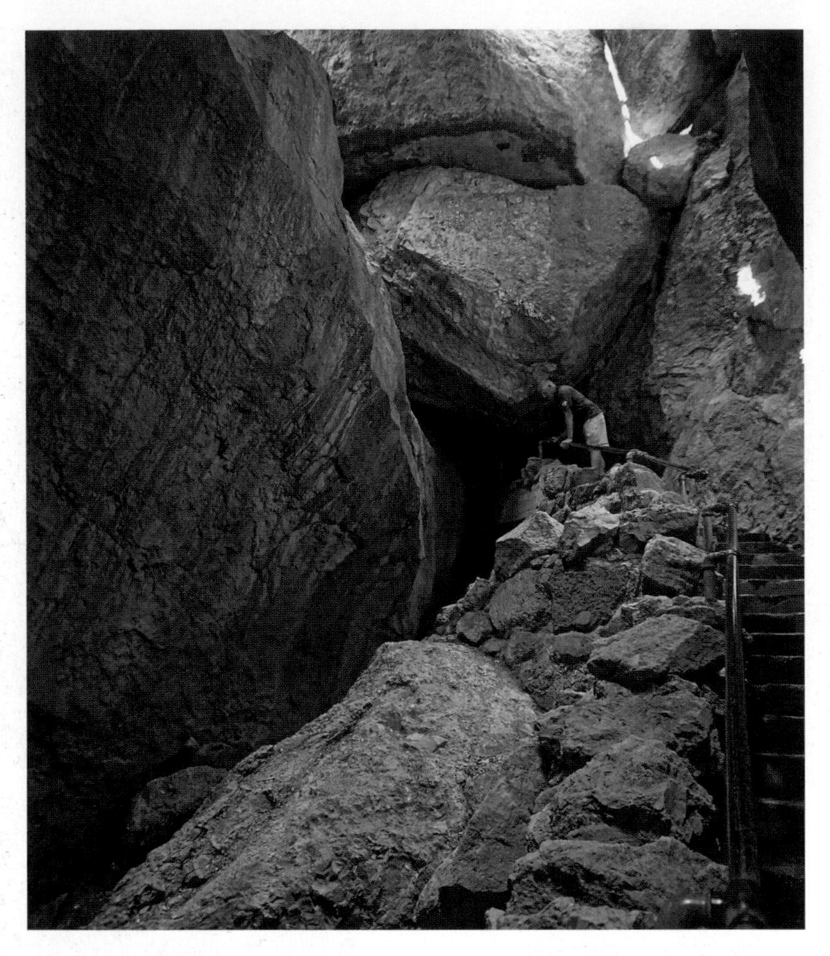

↑ **Turn on your flashlight and prepare to duck your head as you enter the boulder-congested tunnel of Bear Gulch Cave.**

↗ **The startling pink and sage green colors of Pinnacles' volcanic cliffs stand out against a blue sky.**

→ **The largest of all North American flying birds, California condors were nearly wiped out in the 20th century due to the use of the insecticide DDT. Pinnacles National Park plays a large role in recovery efforts.**

are available 32 miles away, in Hollister or Soledad.

## Balconies and Bear Gulch Caves

The park has two sets of talus caves, Balconies and Bear Gulch. To explore them, no spelunking skills are needed, but bring your sense of adventure. At both cave entrances, you turn on a flashlight or headlamp to guide your way, then squeeze through clefts in the rock, duck your head under ledges, and twist and turn through narrow passageways.

Pinnacles' caves are technically not caves at all, but canyons formed by the movement of the San Andreas Fault. Over thousands of years, running water slowly eroded deep, narrow chasms amid the Pinnacles' giant rhyolitic rocks. Huge chunks of these rocks fragmented, broke off and fell into the chasms, occasionally forming a "roof" that created rocky tunnels — talus caves.

Balconies Caves on the park's west side are open daily year-round except after very heavy winter rains. Bear Gulch Caves on the park's east side are closed or partly closed from mid-May to mid-July in order to protect their resident Townsend's big-eared bats. Most of the rest of the year, the cave's lower region is open, and for a short period every March and October, the entire network is open.

## Hike the High Peaks

Pinnacles' most exciting hike is the trek to the High Peaks, a series of jagged pinnacles and spires that can be seen from miles away. A narrow path wanders through this multicolored volcanic labyrinth. Steel guardrails protect hikers from steep drop-offs, and handholds and footholds are blasted into the rock. The route is

a marvel of trail building completed by the Civilian Conservation Corps in the 1930s. Alternatively, take the Tunnel Trail, which bypasses the most treacherous stretch with a 100-foot-long tunnel.

The highest of the High Peaks sits at 2,720 feet, offering a view of the park's undulating grasslands and colorful volcanic monoliths. From this perch, you have a good chance of seeing California condors flying overhead.

With a wingspan of more than 9 feet, condors are the largest of all North American land birds. But their awesome size didn't protect them from near-extinction — by 1987 only 22 California condors remained in the world. In 2003, Pinnacles National Park became an official condor recovery site. It's now the only national park unit that manages a release site for captive-bred California condors.

For your best chance to see condors at Pinnacles, hike to the High Peaks in the early morning or early evening. Condors can also be seen on the ridge just southeast of the park's campground, where they soar on the thermals. Two spotting scopes are set up in the campground near Pinnacles Visitor Center.

# Point Lobos State Natural Reserve

***A jagged shoreline of aquamarine coves, wave-sculpted tide pools, pocket beaches and balletic cypress trees***

## Hot Spot Highlights

- Walk through a grove of windswept Monterey cypress.
- See sea lions and harbor seals on offshore rocks.
- Observe nesting cormorants at Bird Island.
- Scan the seas for whales.

**Address:** Paint Lobos State Natural Reserve, Hwy 1 and Riley Ranch Road, Carmel, CA
**Tel.:** (831) 624-4909
**Websites:** www.pointlobos.org, www.parks.ca.gov/?page_id=571

**Day use only**

**Best season:**
Year-round

**↗ Point Lobos' ocean-worn headlands have been battered by waves for eons.**

One of the crown jewels of the California State Park system, Point Lobos is a 1,250-acre coastal wonderland just south of Carmel and north of Big Sur. Relentless surf and wild winds have pounded this cypress-forested shoreline for millennia. Much of this park's beauty can be enjoyed right from your car window, or with an easy stroll to an overlook point. Just by glancing out toward the sea, visitors have a near-guarantee of spotting sea lions, seals, sea otters, or gray or humpback whales. More than 250 different animal and bird species, plus more than 350 plant species, have been identified at the reserve.

Hikers can choose from crisscrossing trails that travel through groves of Monterey cypress and pines. Start from the Sea Lion Point parking area and walk a gentle loop on Cypress Grove Trail and North Shore Trail.

Start by heading out on the wheelchair-accessible Sea Lion Point Trail to see the barking "sea wolves" that have given this park its name ("lobo" is Spanish for wolf). Then wander along Cypress Grove Trail to see one of only two naturally growing Monterey cypress groves in the world. These gnarled, old-growth trees have been wind-sculpted into surreal shapes. Many have limbs that are decorated with a velvety orange algae called trentepohlia. Its color comes from carotene, the same pigment that occurs in carrots.

Take a side-trip to Whaler's Knoll, where early 20th-century whalers would scan the seas for whales, then hang a signal flag to alert the whaling crew. Today, this high point delivers one of the best views in the park and, in winter, a great chance of whale sightings. In spring, colorful wildflowers brighten the seaside bluffs and shady

**↑ Stately and romantic, these ancient Monterey cypress trees hold their own against the ocean wind.**

**↖ Rusty-red trentepohlia is an algae that grows in very few places on earth. It doesn't affect the health of the cypress trees it attaches to.**

**↖↖ Dudleya succulents decorate Point Lobos' rocky crevices, creating a natural rock garden that might have been designed by a landscape architect.**

↑ **Easy hiking paths at Point Lobos make this park ideal for wildlife watching, botanizing and nature study.**

↗ **Brandt's cormorants colonize Bird Island during spring and summer.**

→ **Small, protected coves make perfect haul-out spots for harbor seals and sea lions.**

forests. The best viewing time is late April and early May.

To learn more about this region's whaling past, bone up on history at the Whalers Cabin Museum, constructed by Chinese fishermen in the 1850s. Exhibits focus on shore whaling; displays include harpoons and whale-oil barrels.

Several more paths are worth exploring: on the park's south end, park at the Bird Island Trailhead and walk an easy 2 miles past two gorgeous craggy coves to view Bird Island, home to a Brandt's cormorant colony in spring and summer. These black birds with bright-blue chins nest right on top of the rock. Guillemots, oystercatchers and brown pelicans may be perched among them.

Alternatively, follow South Shore Trail as it skirts the jagged coastline from China Cove to Sand Hill Cove, passing four tiny coves along the way — Hidden Beach, Weston Beach, The Slot, and Sand Hill Cove. In each of these, you may spot sea otters frolicking in the calm waters.

Still, you can visit only about half of the reserve on foot. The underwater world just offshore is one of California's

richest marine habitats and a state-designated "underwater park." Scuba divers explore the watery world of 70-foot-high kelp forests, where animals without backbones and plants without roots reside in the subdued light under the waves. Divers in Bluefish Cove and Whalers Cove may see lingcod, cabezone and rockfish swimming in and out of the kelp. Diving permits are required, and only a limited number are available each day.

Not surprisingly, Point Lobos is an incredibly popular park. Arrive early in the day, especially in summer, to avoid long lines at the entrance station. Park rangers carefully limit the number of cars that enter the park to avoid overcrowding.

# Big Sur Coast

***A cliff-hanging shoreline that's home to age-old, sky-high redwoods and one of the world's most spectacular highways***

## Hot Spot Highlights

- Hike to waterfalls that cascade in redwood forests and drop to the Pacific.
- See Pfeiffer Beach's famous rock arch and sculpted outcrops.
- Spot gray whales, sea lions and sea otters from high coastal overlooks.

**Address**: Big Sur Station, 47555 Hwy 1, Big Sur, CA
**Tel.**: (831) 667-2315
**Website**: www.parks.ca.gov/?page_id=29838

**Best season:**
Year-round

**↗ Point Sur Lightstation has been presiding over Big Sur's Graveyard of the Pacific since 1889.**

Poet and Big Sur resident Robinson Jeffers described this redwood and rock coast as "that jagged country which nothing but a falling meteor will ever plow." Author Henry Miller, another Big Sur literary celebrity, called it "the face of the earth as the creator intended it to look." A favored spot for painters, poets and creators of all kinds, Big Sur as a specific geographical "place" is hard to define. The name applies to a town, a valley, a river and the entire coastline from just south of Carmel to somewhere north of San Simeon — a distance of about 70 miles.

Only one major road accesses Big Sur, California's Highway 1, the state's first scenic highway. The road snakes alongside the cliff-hanging coastline, slips around the prominent ribs of the Santa Lucia Mountains, slides into dark wooded canyons and soars across graceful bridges. Driving this edge-hugging road means gliding around tight turns with steep drop-offs and striving to keep your eyes on the pavement, despite the never-ending allure of coastal vistas.

The "town" part of Big Sur

↑ **At Bixby Bridge, magnificent spikes of purple "pride of Madeira" welcome visitors to the Big Sur Coast.**

includes the area's famous and fabulous inns and restaurants: the Ventana Inn, the Post Ranch Inn, Nepenthe and Deetjen's. Several state parks and private campgrounds offer places to pitch your tent or park your RV. Be sure to make lodging and camping reservations in advance, as Big Sur is deservedly popular.

## Point Sur Lightstation

Atop Point Sur stands the Point Sur Lightstation, an 1889 stone sentinel presiding over the shipwreck site once known as the "Graveyard of the Pacific." Back in the days when the only way to get here was on horseback, 395 wooden steps led to the lighthouse, originally a giant multi-wick kerosene lantern surrounded by a Fresnel lens with a 16-panel prism. This 34-acre area, with its central rocky mound, is now a state historic park and a great place for enjoying coastal views and spotting gray whales during their winter and spring migration. Entrance to the park and lighthouse is by guided tour only (www.pointsur.org).

↑ **Beautiful Pfeiffer Beach features wave-washed blowholes and arches and a beach highlighted by mauve-and-black sand.**

## Pfeiffer Beach

Due to the precipitous cliffs and rocky shores that line the Big Sur coast, the only easily accessible beach in Big Sur proper is Pfeiffer Beach, a mile-long stretch of sand that is bounded by a forest of cypress trees and offshore rock formations with craggy caves, blowholes and arches. Its soft white sand is streaked with mauve and black, resulting from eroding minerals in its bluffs. Not surprisingly, this is a popular spot for photographers. The beach is reached via a narrow, 2-mile-long access road, 1 mile south of Pfeiffer Big Sur State Park. Swimming is not recommended: the water is cold, the surf capricious and riptides deadly.

## Andrew Molera State Park

This coastside state park on Big Sur's northern edge has plenty to offer for hikers and beach lovers. An easy 1.25-mile trail leads from the main parking lot to the windswept promontory at Molera Point, an ideal high spot to watch for passing whales and dolphins and count the sea lions lying on Molera Beach's rocks. Or, cross the footbridge over the Big Sur River and follow Beach Trail for a mile to Molera Beach. Just before the beach, the Bluffs Trail cuts off to the left, paralleling the coast on a nearly level course and offering nonstop ocean views. About 2.5 miles out, near a junction with Panorama Trail, a short cutoff called Spring Trail leads to an exquisite stretch of driftwood-laden beach.

## Pfeiffer Big Sur State Park

A favorite spot for camping, this park is also a fine place for hiking or swimming in the Big Sur River. Most visitors walk all or part of the 2-mile Pfeiffer Falls and Valley View Loop to enjoy the redwood forest and see the park's 60-foot waterfall, a fern-lined cataract at its best in spring and early summer. If you'd like more exercise, backtrack about 100 feet from the falls and follow Valley View Trail as it climbs up and out of the canyon to a high overlook of the Big Sur Valley and Point Sur. Or hike the Buzzard's Roost Overlook Trail, which begins near the Big Sur River, then ascends out of the redwoods and onto higher, chaparral-covered slopes. From high on Pfeiffer Ridge, you'll enjoy a 360-degree view of the Pacific Ocean, the Big Sur River gorge and the Santa Lucia Mountains.

**↑ The Big Sur River is a fine place to cool your feet under the shade of alders and maples.**

**↖ Sixty-foot-tall Pfeiffer Falls is a mere trickle in early autumn but flows with vigor after winter and spring rains.**

↑ **Walk to the relics of Partington's historic doghole port and you might just spot a sea otter floating in the kelp beds.**

↗ **The image of graceful McWay Falls plummeting to the sand has appeared on countless calendars and postcards.**

## Julia Pfeiffer Burns State Park

One of California's most photographed waterfalls plummets to the sea at McWay Cove, and you can see it with only a quarter-mile walk. The wheelchair-accessible McWay Falls Overlook Trail leads through a culvert under the highway and out to the cliffs near Saddle Rock, where the waterfall plunges to the sand and then flows to the Pacific.

Two miles north on Highway 1 is the park's Partington Cove Trailhead. From the gate by the highway, the Partington Point Trail leads a steep half mile down to a fork. The right path leads to a tiny rock-strewn beach at Partington Creek's mouth; the left path leads into the redwoods, across a wooden footbridge and through a

↑ **California's coast redwoods meet their southernmost habitat at Limekiln State Park, where four 1880s lime kilns are nearly hidden in the forest.**

rock tunnel built in the 1880s by pioneer John Partington. On the tunnel's far side is the remains of an old port, where lumber was loaded onto seagoing freighters. This is a great spot to scan the cobalt waters for sea otters, which favor this rock-sheltered cove.

## Limekiln State Park

About 2.5 miles south of Lucia, this 700-acre state park preserves some of the oldest, largest and most vigorous redwoods in Monterey County. The park is named for its 1880s wood-fired kilns, which smelted quarried limestone into powdered lime, a critical ingredient for bricks and cement. Four still-standing kilns can be seen via a 1-mile walk through the redwoods. In the wet season, be sure to take the right fork just beyond the second footbridge, which leads to Limekiln Falls, a spectacular 100-foot waterfall that drops over a limestone face. Getting to the waterfall requires some boulder-hopping, and in spring, you may end up with wet feet, but it's good fun.

# Carrizo Plain National Monument

***The largest native grasslands remaining in California, where tule elk and pronghorn roam freely***

### Hot Spot Highlights

- See pronghorn and tule elk graze the grasslands.
- Marvel at 3,000-year-old Native American pictographs.
- Witness a spectacular spring wildflower show.

**Address**: Carrizo Plain National Monument, 17495 Soda Lake Road, California Valley, CA
**Tel.**: (661) 391-6000 or (805) 475-2131
**Website**: www.ca.blm.gov/carrizo

**Best season:**
Late March and early April for wildflowers; autumn for migrating birds

**↗ The pronghorn is known for its incredible speed, which can top 55 miles per hour.**

Sixty miles east of San Luis Obispo via narrow, two-lane roads, lie the grasslands and wildflower plains of Carrizo Plain National Monument. To wander in Carrizo Plain is like stepping back in time to the California of three centuries ago, when thousands of pronghorn and elk grazed the region's vast savannahs. These graceful, grazing ungulates faced near-extinction in the late 1800s due to habitat loss and indiscriminate hunting.

Both species were reintroduced to this region in the late 20th century. Majestic tule elk have been successfully reintroduced at several California locations, including Point

↑ **In March and April, the hills and grasslands of Carrizo Plain explode in a kaleidoscope of colorful flowers.**

Reyes National Seashore and Tule Elk State Natural Reserve. But the cinnamon-colored pronghorn — often mistakenly called antelope — are rarer. These uniquely North American mammals (no relation to the African antelope) are best known for their incredible speed, which can top 55 miles per hour, second only to the cheetah's speed. Carrizo Plain's herd was transported from northeastern California in 1990. Carrizo's grass-covered plains, sometimes called "California's Serengeti," are also the last refuge for disappearing species like the San Joaquin kit fox, San Joaquin antelope squirrel, burrowing owl, giant kangaroo rat and blunt-nosed leopard lizard.

Where there are grasslands, there are wildflowers, and nowhere in California is this more apparent than at Carrizo Plain. From mid-March to mid-April in a good flower year, the plains are nearly smothered in fields of tidy tips, owl's clover and California poppies. During 2017's rare "superbloom"

↑ **The wildflower show at Carrizo Plain varies every year depending on rainfall and other environmental factors, but in peak years, it's a splashy pageant.**

wildflower season, the rounded hills were transformed by a phantasmagoric palette of yellow, purple and orange, attracting thousands of photographers. Every year, flower experts show up here in search of rare and endangered species such as San Joaquin woolly threads (tiny yellow flowers), Kern mallow (delicate pink), pale-yellow layia and Munz's tidy tips. The showiest of the monument's endangered plants is California jewelflower, its wine-colored buds opening into white flowers.

At the monument's north end is Soda Lake, a 3,000-acre expanse that comprises one of the largest remaining alkaline wetlands left in California. The lake is completely dry for most of the year, looking like a glistening white bed of crusty salt, but after winter rains flood the salt flats, migrating birds congregate on the wind-ruffled waters. Shorebirds, including thousands of sandhill cranes, depend on the seasonal briny water.

Carrizo Plain is in a remote area in Central California,

about 50 miles from the nearest large town. Stock up your car with gas, snacks and water (available in Maricopa and Santa Margarita). The monument has two developed campgrounds: KCL and Selby. Dispersed or primitive camping is also permitted in some areas of the monument.

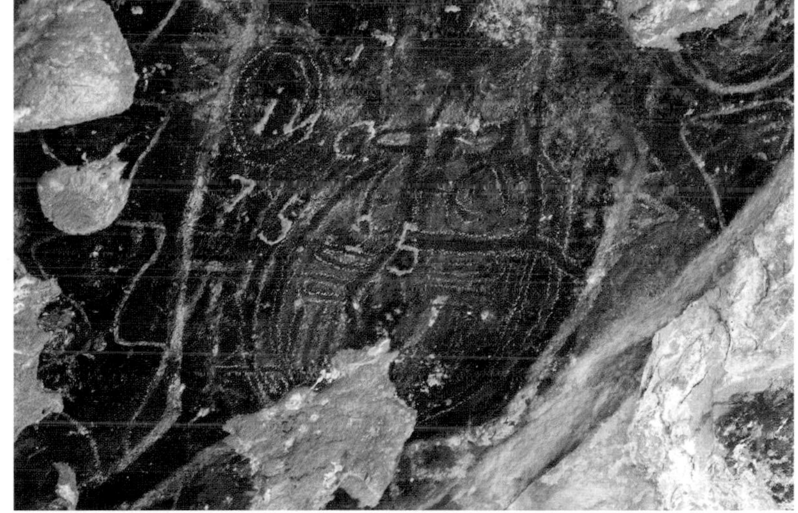

↑ **The sandstone amphitheater at Painted Rock is etched with Chumash Indian paintings dating back 3,000 years.**

↖ **Three-thousand-acre Soda Lake is one of the largest remaining alkaline wetlands in California.**

## Painted Rock

Soda Lake and the surrounding grasslands are spectacular enough, but if you've driven all the way out to Carrizo Plain, you must see Painted Rock, a rounded sandstone amphitheater that has some of the most significant Native American pictographs in the country. The 55-foot-high rock is covered in 3,000-year-old Chumash Indian paintings, including geometric designs as well as human figures, snakes and aquatic images. Reserve a permit or guided hike at www.recreation.gov. The site is closed for self-guided hikes from March 1 to July 15 to protect nesting birds.

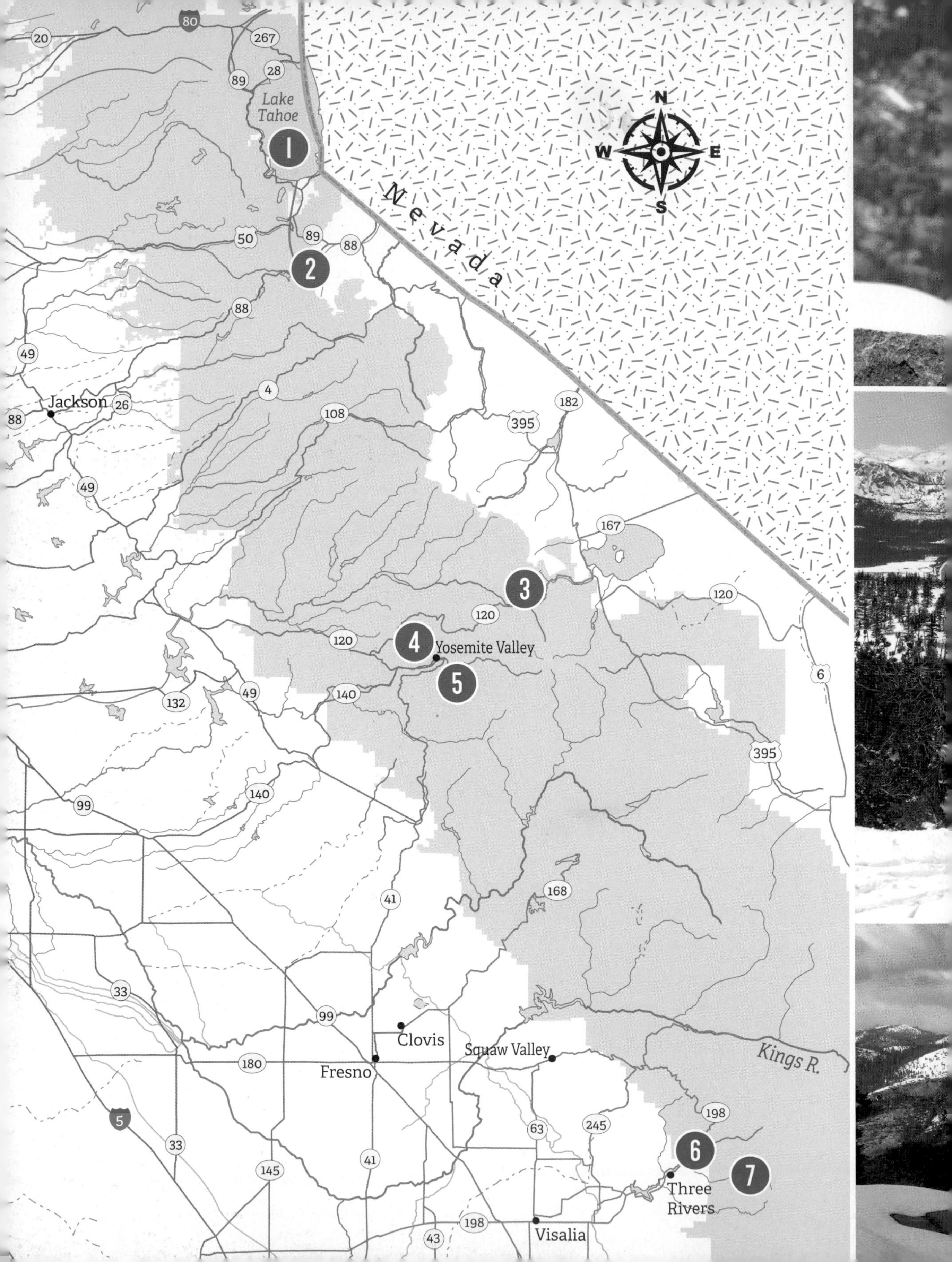

Lake Tahoe
Nevada
N
S
E
W
1
2
3
4
5
6
7
Jackson
Yosemite Valley
Clovis
Squaw Valley
Fresno
Kings R.
Three Rivers
Visalia
80
20
267
28
89
50
88
49
4
26
108
395
182
167
120
6
140
132
99
41
168
33
180
5
63
245
198
145
43

# Western Sierra Nevada

# Lake Tahoe and Desolation Wilderness

***One of America's deepest and purest alpine lakes offers year-round outdoor recreation***

## Hot Spot Highlights

- Sightsee, swim, kayak, camp and fish at North America's largest alpine lake.
- Ski or snowboard at one of 14 ski resorts.
- Hike to glacially sculpted lakes and peaks in Desolation Wilderness.

**Address**: Lake Tahoe is 110 miles east of Sacramento via Hwy 50 or Interstate 80
**Tel.**: (530) 581-6900 or (775) 588-4591
**Website**: https://visitinglaketahoe.com

**Best season:**
Year-round

↗ **Purple shooting stars fill wet alpine meadows with their brilliant colors. The flowers point downward after they are pollinated.**

↗↗ **Northern flickers drum into wood with their beaks to communicate and mark their territory — often to the dismay of Tahoe homeowners.**

The Lake Tahoe region is clearly defined by its 22-mile-long, azure-blue lake — "a noble sheet of blue water lifted 6,300 feet above the level of the sea, and walled in by a rim of snow-clad peaks," as Mark Twain wrote in 1871. The lake can fill a record book with its statistics — it's the 10th-deepest lake in the world at 1,645 feet, the second-deepest in the United States after Crater Lake, and it boasts 72 miles of shoreline, two-thirds of which lie in California and the rest in Nevada. It's also one of the purest lakes in the world, with 99.994 percent purity — roughly the same as distilled water.

It's not Tahoe's numbers but rather its images that linger — an osprey diving into a calm cove, a black bear drinking water at the lake's edge, the setting sun lingering behind Mount Tallac, a rosy pink alpenglow lighting up snow-covered slopes.

Small cities line the lake's north shore and south shore, providing anything a visitor might need or want. Emerald Bay Road (Highway 89) travels along the quieter west shore, providing access to several stunning vista points and hiking trails. At the Inspiration Point overlook, drivers stop to snap photos of Emerald Bay, its sparkling

↑ Lake Tahoe is known for its remarkable water clarity. It's possible to see a Secchi dish (a measuring instrument that looks like a dinner plate) 70 to 75 feet below the surface.

→ Lake Tahoe's only island — pine-clad Fannette in Emerald Bay — houses a single structure, a crumbling 1929 teahouse.

blue waters punctuated by rugged Fannette Island. At the Vikingsholm Trailhead, an easy trail leads to the lakeshore, where you can dip your toes into Emerald Bay's cobalt water, or rent a kayak or standup paddleboard to paddle out to Fannette Island. At Emerald Bay State Park, the 7-mile Rubicon Trail travels along the lakeshore under the shade of pines and firs. Bald eagles and ospreys nest in tall trees near the water.

Trails also head away

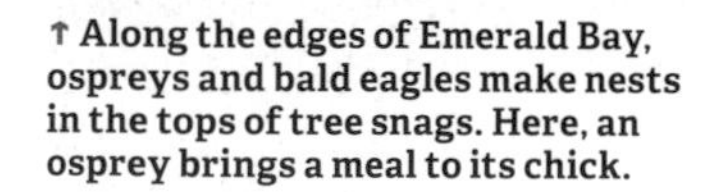

↑ **Along the edges of Emerald Bay, ospreys and bald eagles make nests in the tops of tree snags. Here, an osprey brings a meal to its chick.**

↑↑ **Paddling a kayak is one of the best ways to see Lake Tahoe. A designated "Water Trail" with 20 separate entry points covers 72 miles around the lake.**

↗ **In the spring and early summer months, Tahoe's waterfalls cascade over shelves of smooth granite, fueled by melting snow.**

from the massive lake into Desolation Wilderness, one of the Sierra Nevada's most stunning glacier-sculpted landscapes. The wilderness area's 64,000 acres of subalpine and alpine forest, granite-bound lakes and peaks, and wildflower-filled meadows offer hundreds of worthwhile destinations. One of the most popular is the summit of 9,735-foot Mount Tallac, a metamorphic peak that towers over the Tahoe basin. This challenging 9-mile hike (3,400 feet of elevation gain) starts out deceivingly easy as it climbs a glacial moraine that hems in beautiful Fallen Leaf Lake. The trail passes pond-like Floating Island Lake, then a mile later, rockbound Cathedral Lake. Beyond the small lakes, a punishing climb begins. The trail traverses to

Tallac's southwest side, then ascends the jagged summit block. On top, a rewarding vista takes in all of Lake Tahoe to the east and north and a wild expanse of Desolation Wilderness to the west.

For lake lovers, the Desolation Wilderness offers a bonanza of choices — but they all come with a climb. The trailheads at Eagle Falls and Bayview Campground provide easy access from Emerald Bay Road. Dick's Lake, set in a dramatic glacial cirque with 9,974-foot Dick's Peak soaring behind it, makes a perfect day-long trek or short overnight backpacking trip. The trail begins with a steep 850-foot ascent to Granite Lake. Catch your breath at an overlook where the trail breaks out of the conifers to expose broad views of Emerald Bay, Cascade Lake and Lake Tahoe. Shortly beyond lies Granite Lake, another good rest stop before the next steep ascent to the ridge near Maggie's Peaks. From here, the grade mercifully levels out. At the Dick's Lake junction, turn left and climb gently over a series of low, glacially carved ridges and basins, where it's easy to imagine the Ice Age flows advancing and carving out the rounded peaks and polished canyons. The granite-lined shore of Dick's Lake is ideal for picnicking and sunbathing.

Long-distance hikers will be tempted by the Tahoe Rim Trail (TRT), a 165-mile path that traverses the ridgeline of Lake Tahoe's crown of peaks. From mid-June through October, the trail offers a multitude of

**↑ Viewed from the west side of Mount Tallac, Pyramid Peak towers above Aloha Lake in Desolation Wilderness.**

**↓ Day-hikers and backpackers can choose from hundreds of lake destinations in Desolation Wilderness, including hemlock-lined Dicks Lake.**

day-hiking and backpacking options. The TRT winds its way through valleys, along ridges, and up the granite peaks of the Carson Range and Desolation Wilderness, overlapping at several points with the 2,650-mile Pacific Crest Trail.

In winter, Tahoe is Northern California's favorite

place to play in the snow, whether your sport is alpine skiing, cross-country skiing, snowboarding, snowshoeing, snowmobiling or sledding. Snow may fall as early as November, and in some years, the spring melt holds off until June. Fourteen ski resorts dot the lake's shoreline, from mega-resorts like Squaw Valley, Northstar and Heavenly to much smaller, family-run ski hills. Also near the lake is Royal Gorge, North America's largest cross-country ski resort, offering 100 groomed trails for cross-country striders, skate skiers and snowshoers.

**↑ Heavenly Ski Resort on Tahoe's South Shore offers expansive views of the lake from south to north — a length of 22 miles.**

**← On a bluebird powder day in Lake Tahoe, the slopeside trees are flocked in white.**

# Carson Pass

***A volcanic landscape shows off spectacular summer wildflowers and brilliant autumn colors***

## Hot Spot Highlights

- Walk the High Sierra's premier wildflower trail.
- See blazing autumn aspen groves.
- Hike across a volcanic landscape to dozens of alpine lakes.
- Ski, snowboard or snowshoe on groomed trails or backcountry terrain.

**Address**: Carson Pass Information Station, Hwy 88 at Carson Pass (60 miles east of Jackson, CA)
**Tel.**: (209) 258-8606
**Website**: www.enfia.org/hwy-88-carson-pass

**Best season:**
Year-round

↗ **Indian paintbrush comes in myriad colors, but the most common shade at Carson Pass is this coral red.**

↗↗ **The volcanic soils in this High Sierra region contribute to the vibrant flower tapestry.**

Less than an hour's drive from bustling Lake Tahoe, Carson Pass feels like a world apart. Named for the famous scout and explorer Kit Carson, this alpine region is still blissfully undeveloped. A few scattered cabin resorts, a handful of restaurants, and one ski area comprise the only visitor services in a 30-square-mile area. The top of the Highway 88 pass at 8,600 feet is the cornerstone for outdoor recreation in Alpine County, which has only two residents per square mile.

Sierra lovers flock here in summer for hiking, mountain biking and some of the best fishing anywhere in these mountains, with hungry trout lurking in more than 60 lakes, numerous streams and the world-famous Carson River. Savvy hikers know Carson Pass has one of the Sierra's most colorful summer wildflower shows and one of the most dramatic autumn leaf displays. Volcanic peaks, alpine lakes, aspen groves and river-cut meadows wait to be explored.

In summer, make your first stop at the Carson Pass Information Station, a small log cabin at the top of Carson Pass. Here, the contorted trunks of lodgepole pines hint at the heavy snow that falls each winter. The Pacific Crest Trail (PCT) passes through, heading north toward Tahoe and south

↑ **Hikers head toward Winnemucca Lake to witness Carson Pass' annual display of alpine wildflowers. The colors usually peak in mid- to late July.**

toward Yosemite, offering several excellent short hikes. Traveling south from the pass, the trail makes a short climb through the forest, then departs the trees and opens out to a striking volcanic landscape. During July, the peak of the wildflower season, you'll be wowed by waist-high lupine and seemingly endless acres of mule's ears growing in the volcanic soil. Turquoise-colored Frog Lake is just off the trail, framed by the distinct outline of Elephant's Back, an old lava dome. The best flowers show themselves in the next 1.5 miles. The trail skirts open meadows lined with volcanic soil that produces a vibrant botanical tapestry. Scarlet gilia, Indian paintbrush, blue flax and sierra lilies are prolific. Where tiny streams flow across the path, lupine, columbine and monkeyflower grow in profusion.

The trail deposits you at photogenic Winnemucca Lake, a blue-green gem whose shoreline is dotted with clusters of whitebark pines and hemlocks. Another steep mile uphill is Round Top Lake, set directly below 10,381-foot Round Top Peak in a deeply carved glacial cirque. Sure-footed hikers can summit Round Top Peak by following a footpath from the lake's east end. The last 50 yards to the summit require a third-class scramble, so climb only as high as your comfort level allows. The volcanic peak's knife-thin ridge offers dazzling vistas. To the north lies Lake Tahoe, Caples Lake, Woods Lake, Round Top Lake, Winnemucca Lake

**↑ Jeffrey pines and western junipers cast slim shadows over the sparkling, gem-like lakes that border Highway 88.**

**→ At Carson Pass, it's hard to decide which seasonal show is more captivating — the autumn aspen extravaganza or the summer wildflower spectacle.**

and Frog Lake. Even more dramatic is the southward vista of deep and immense Summit City Canyon, 3,000 feet below. On the clearest days, Mount Diablo in the San Francisco Bay Area, 100 miles to the west, can be seen.

In the autumn months, diminishing daylight hours and cooler temperatures send a message to the dense aspen groves near Carson Pass. Photosynthesis works its chemical magic, and the trees unfurl their colors, offering up a leafy bounty of glowing golds, opulent oranges and traffic-stopping reds. On the west side of the highway pass, Hope Valley (near the junction of Highways 88 and 89) is one of the best aspen-viewing spots. On the east side, the groves near Caples Lake, Silver Lake and Woods Lake offer first-rate fall colors.

Winter at Carson Pass also has its charms — the region is renowned for its deep and consistent snowfall, up to 700 inches per year. The steep volcanic landscape lends itself to cross-country skiing, alpine skiing, and snowboarding at Kirkwood Ski Resort. For the intrepid skier or snowshoer who prefers trackless snow, miles of backcountry terrain lie just off the highway.

YOSEMITE NATIONAL PARK

# Tuolumne Meadows

***The Sierra Nevada's largest subalpine meadow is a playground of granite domes, gemlike lakes, verdant meadows and river waterfalls***

## Hot Spot Highlights

- Ascend a 13,503-foot peak.
- Wallow in the scenery at high-alpine lakes.
- See waterfalls along the Tuolumne River.
- Climb to the top of a glacially polished dome.

**Address**: Tuolumne Meadows Visitor Center, Hwy 120/Tioga Pass Road, Yosemite, CA
**Tel.**: (209) 372-0200
**Website**: www.nps.gov/yose

**Best season:**
June to October

! Roads are not plowed in winter

**↗ Near Olmsted Point, granite slabs are gussied-up with pink mountain pride penstemon.**

One of the most photographed regions of Yosemite, Tuolumne Meadow's wide, grassy expanse is bounded by high granite domes and peaks. At 8,600 feet in elevation, this pristine meadow extends for more than 2 miles along the Tuolumne River, making it the largest subalpine meadow in the Sierra Nevada. Lace up your boots and wander easy meadow trails or rugged paths to the summits of lofty domes and granite-backed alpine lakes.

### Soda Springs

On the meadow's north side, take a walk to this permanent spring, where carbonated water bubbles up from iron-tinted soil. You'll get a look at Tuolumne Meadow's abundant wildflowers, grasses and sedges, plus a glimpse into the area's history. This is the spot where conservationist John Muir and editor Robert Underwood Johnson discussed the idea of creating Yosemite National Park. The Sierra Club purchased this beautiful stretch of meadow

↑ Lembert Dome rises above the Tuolumne River, luring rock climbers to its vertical side and hikers to its sloping back side.

so it could never be developed, and later donated it to the National Park Service. The club's Parsons Memorial Lodge was built here in 1915, and to this day the beautiful timber-and-stone structure serves as a public gathering place. Every summer, scientists, writers, artists and musicians give free presentations here.

## Lembert Dome and Dog Lake

This glacially polished rock is an example of a *rôche moutonnée*, a dome with one gently sloping side and one side that drops off steeply. Rock climbers tackle Lembert Dome's south escarpment, but hikers can follow the trail around its east side and up to the bald dome's 9,450-foot summit. The reward is an astonishing view of Tuolumne Meadows and surrounding peaks, plus the chance to walk on Yosemite's surprisingly "grippy" granite. The dome was named for Jean Baptiste Lembert, a homesteader who lived in Tuolumne Meadows in the mid-1880s. A short distance from the dome is lovely Dog Lake, where bald eagles often circle above, looking for trout. This is a fine spot to soak

↑ **In autumn, Tuolumne's grasses turn tawny gold, soon to be buried under snow for a solid five months.**

↗ **Elizabeth Lake, nestled beneath Unicorn Peak's granite spire, is an easy hike from Tuolumne Meadows Campground.**

your feet on a warm summer day. At 9,170 feet elevation, the lake is wide, shallow and deep blue. Two massive peaks line its backdrop — Mount Dana and Mount Gibbs.

## Pothole Dome

On the western edge of Tuolumne Meadows lies Pothole Dome, a low granite dome that makes an easy, rewarding hike. A trail parallels Tioga Road for about 100 feet to a stand of trees; the dome lies just beyond. Pick any route you like and head uphill. In less than 15 minutes, you can be on top of Pothole Dome, gazing at a fine view of Lembert Dome, Mount Dana, Mount Gibbs and, of course, Tuolumne Meadows and its namesake river. To discover more of this beautiful area, hike back down the dome and continue on the trail alongside the meadow leading north to the Tuolumne River. In this stretch, the watercourse drops in a series of photogenic cascades.

## Elizabeth Lake

Starting at the trailhead elevation of 8,600 feet, you have a mere 1,000-foot elevation gain over 2.25 miles to get to lovely Elizabeth Lake, set in a basin at the foot of distinctive Unicorn Peak. Some visitors swim or fish here, others try to climb Unicorn Peak (10,900 feet), but most are happy

to sit near the lake's edge and admire the views of the sculpted peak and its neighbors in the Cathedral Range. (Trailhead is located near the group campsite at Tuolumne Meadows Campground.)

## Middle and Upper Gaylor Lakes

The Gaylor Lakes trail leads to two startlingly beautiful glacial lakes above 10,000 feet in elevation. The path begins near Yosemite's Tioga Pass entrance station, then climbs a short but steep ridge and drops down to the middle lake. From Middle Gaylor Lake, follow the creek gently uphill to the east for 1 mile to reach smaller Upper Gaylor Lake. A trail skirts around its north side and heads uphill for a few hundred yards to the site of the Great Sierra Mine and the remains of an old stone cabin. The twin Granite Lakes, tucked in below a massive granite cirque, lie about three-quarters of a mile northwest of Middle Gaylor Lake. Although there is no formal trail to the Granite Lakes, it's an easy cross-country ramble to the site.

## Cathedral Lakes

The two Cathedral Lakes are set within a classic glacial cirque, tucked in below 10,840-foot Cathedral Peak. The trail departs Tioga Pass Road and follows the John

**↑ In the 1880s, gold and silver miners failed to strike it rich in the high country near Gaylor Lake, but today treasure is easy to find in this stark Sierra scenery.**

**↓ Crystalline lakes and tiny alpine wildflowers are found on every trail near 10,000-foot Tioga Pass.**

Muir Trail for 3.2 miles, climbing steeply much of the way. As the path breaks out of the trees, you'll gain a view of distinctive Cathedral Peak, a swooping granite pinnacle that's popular for rock climbing. At 3.2 miles, turn right on the Cathedral Lake spur to reach the lower, larger lake in half a mile. You'll follow the lake's inlet stream through a gorgeous meadow to the water's edge. Many hikers stop here and go no farther, but it's a pity not to see Upper Cathedral Lake as well. To reach it, retrace your steps to the John Muir Trail and continue another half a mile. Fishing is often better in the upper lake, and the scenery is even more sublime. Campsites are

found close to the lakes, but you need to secure a wilderness permit far in advance in order to spend the night.

## Mount Dana

Summiting Mount Dana is a rite of passage for many Yosemite hikers. The path to the top of the 13,053-foot peak requires a 3,100-foot elevation gain condensed into a mere 3 miles. The trek begins near the Tioga Pass entrance station with a pleasant ramble through Dana Meadows and then a dense lodgepole pine forest. Soon the grade becomes more intense, but this first stretch is highlighted by a spectacular wildflower show that usually peaks in late July. Lupine, larkspur, Indian paintbrush, senecio — they're all here, in all their glory. The climbing gets tougher in the 2nd mile, but stick with it and soon you'll have climbed above treeline. At the 11,600-foot mark, a giant trail cairn marks a large, rock-covered plateau. You still have another mile

**↑ Purple-blue sky pilot blooms among the rock scree and patches of lingering snow on Mount Dana's summit.**

**↖ The short-but-mercilessly-steep hike to 13,053-foot Mount Dana is a rite of passage for many Yosemite hikers.**

**← Afternoon clouds cast ominous shadows over the sweeping turrets of Cathedral Peak. Upper Cathedral Lake lies just below.**

↑ **Tuolumne Falls is one of four named waterfalls on the Tuolumne River. All of them can be seen by hiking west on the river trail from Tuolumne Meadows.**

and 1,500 feet to go, and it's slow going over a shale-covered slope. There's no shade and plenty of loose rock. But when you finally reach the summit, you are witness to one of the finest views in the Sierras. Your field of vision encompasses Mono, Ellery and Saddlebag lakes, Glacier Canyon, Tuolumne Meadows, Lembert Dome and an untold wealth of high peaks.

A few tips for making the ascent safely: First, wait until mid-July or later to make the trip, as Mount Dana can be snow-covered long into the summer. Second, get an early start in the morning so you have no chance of encountering afternoon thunderstorms. Third, carry (and drink) as much water as you can. Fourth, wear good sunglasses and sun protection at this high elevation. And last, pace yourself to give your body a chance to adjust to the 13,000-foot altitude.

## Glen Aulin and Tuolumne Falls

Yosemite Valley is famous for its free-leaping waterfalls, but Tuolumne Meadows has its own waterworks — a series of whitewater cascades on

↑ **High above the treeline, Vogelsang Lake is home to one of five High Sierra Camps, where backpackers can eat hearty meals and sleep on cots in cozy tent cabins.**

the rollicking Tuolumne River. Hike to them by following the trail alongside the river for 4.5 miles, then veering right at the sign for Glen Aulin. The path descends until it reaches Tuolumne Falls, a long series of boulder-choked cascades. On warm days, you can take a bracing swim in the waterfall's pool, adjacent to Glen Aulin High Sierra Camp — a great place to spend the night if you can score a reservation (www.travelyosemite.com). Turn around here for a 9-mile round-trip, or continue downstream to see more of the Tuolumne River's waterfalls — Le Conte, California and Waterwheel Falls. Tuolumne Meadow's small visitor center, housed in a historic cabin, features exhibits that focus on the area's geology, wildflowers and wildlife. Picnic and hiking supplies can be found at the large canvas tent that is the Tuolumne Meadows Store. Under the same tent is the Tuolumne Meadows Grill, which serves hearty breakfasts and lunches. Nearby, the Tuolumne Meadows Lodge offers overnight accommodations in tent cabins, as well as delicious dinners and breakfasts.

YOSEMITE NATIONAL PARK

# Yosemite Valley

***A granite spectacle carved by glaciers, framed by waterfalls and punctuated by domes and spires***

### Hot Spot Highlights

- See the largest single piece of granite rock on earth — and the climbers who tackle it.
- Climb to the top of the tallest free-leaping waterfall in North America.
- Make the epic trek to Half Dome's bald pate.

**Address**: Yosemite Valley Visitor Center, 9035 Village Drive, Yosemite Valley, CA
**Tel.**: (209) 372-0200
**Website**: www.nps.gov/yose

**Best season:**
Year-round

Seven miles long and 1 mile across at its widest, Yosemite Valley comprises a mélange of verdant meadows and dense forests bisected by the clear Merced River. Even though the valley contains only 1 percent of the park's entire acreage, it's the most visited region of Yosemite National Park. It's a visual and geologic marvel — a 4,000-foot-deep trough lined by towering cliffs and glacially sculpted, polished rock. A long list of geologists, photographers, artists and writers have celebrated its wonders.

A rich tapestry of wildlife, including black bears, mule deer and chipmunks, resides here, as do several hundred people who are employed in the national park. Newcomers may be surprised to find the valley accommodates a small city, including a dentist's office, jail, courtroom, auto garage and church, which are mixed in with visitor services like lodgings, campgrounds and restaurants. The valley's park-managed activities run the gamut, from ranger-led nature walks to ice skating to photography seminars, from Native American basket-making to rock-climbing lessons, from river rafting to watercolor painting. For first-time visitors, the best strategy is simply to head out on a hiking trail or pedal the 12 miles of smooth, paved bike paths tracing the valley floor. You'll be surrounded by nature's marvels in every direction.

## Half Dome

Without question, Yosemite's most recognizable chunk of granite is the sheared-off granite dome known as Half Dome. Several spots on the valley floor offer great views of this iconic rock formation. One is at Mirror Lake, or on the trail just beyond it, where you can stand at the base of the famous stone monolith. Other good viewing spots are at Stoneman Meadow, across the road from Half Dome Village, or at Tunnel View, just above the valley on Highway 41. If you want to join the legion of hikers worldwide who have summited Half Dome, you must reserve a permit far in

↑ **Curvaceous Half Dome is a granite attention-grabber. Its 2,000-foot-high northwest face — the side that appears to be "sheared off" — is just a few degrees shy of being perfectly vertical.**

← **A 440-foot stretch of cables makes it possible for hikers to ascend Half Dome. Without the cables, only rock climbers could make it to the top**

advance (www.recreation.gov), and you must be in great physical shape. The trek is a 16-mile round-trip with a prodigious 4,800 feet of elevation gain. The final summit ascent is aided by steel cables drilled into the rock, and you'll need arm strength as well as leg strength to haul yourself up 440 feet of nearly vertical granite. Day-hikers need to plan on an early morning start to beat the heat and possible afternoon thundershowers (start at 5 a.m.). To make the trip easier, you can backpack in and camp at Little Yosemite Valley (overnight wilderness permit required), saving the final ascent for the next day.

↑ Climbing El Capitan is a multiday endeavor that requires sleeping in a portable hanging tent, or portaledge, with thousands of feet of thin air below you.

← From the banks of the Merced River, Yosemite visitors can look up at El Capitan's massive profile. This gray-tan leviathan is the largest single piece of granite rock on earth.

## El Capitan

Another of Yosemite Valley's famous granite precipices is El Capitan, which geologists consider to be the largest single piece of granite rock on earth. Towering 3,593 feet above the valley floor, it is arguably the most famous rock-climbing site in the world. Since the 1950s, a succession of bold climbers has inched their way to the top. Most do it in 3 to 5 days with nights spent sleeping on ledges or tethered into hammocks (watch for the glimmer of climbers' headlamps as they get ready to tuck in for the night). However, a brazen new breed of "speed climbers" have completed the ascent in only a matter of hours. The current record was set by Alex Honnold and Tommy Caldwell in June 2018. To see the daredevils tackling this granite behemoth, take a seat in El Capitan Meadow along Northside Drive. With a good pair of binoculars, you can easily sit here for hours, watching these athletes make like Spiderman on El Cap's sheer face.

## Mirror Lake

When this lake is at its fullest in late spring, it reflects a lovely mirror image of Mount

↑ **Mirror Lake is not actually a lake, but rather a pool on Tenaya Creek. Every spring, it fills with water from melting snow, creating a mirrorlike reflection of Half Dome and its granite neighbors.**

↗ **A few miles up the Mist Trail, the 317-foot-tall curtain of Vernal Fall plummets downcanyon, casting rainbows in the afternoon sun.**

→ **The best way to see Yosemite Valley is to get out of your car. Walk, ride a bike or, best of all, paddle an inflatable raft down the Merced River.**

Watkins, a granite summit named for one of Yosemite's earliest photographers. A brief interpretive loop trail gives you a look into Yosemite's natural history and also its history as a world-famous park. The lake is actually not a lake at all, but a pool on Tenaya Creek that is slowly filling with sediment. By late summer each year, it looks more like a meadow than a lake, although autumn's first rains will fill it to the brim once more. In the 1880s the lake was dammed, and a bathhouse was built on its edges; park visitors floated around its surface in small rowboats.

## Waterfalls

Among Yosemite's many bragging rights, its waterfalls rank near the top. Yosemite Falls holds the undisputed title of the tallest waterfall in North America. The upper, lower and middle falls combined top out at a prodigious 2,425 feet. It's a strenuous 7.4-mile hike to reach the top of the upper fall, but the base of the lower fall can be visited via an easy, level stroll of a few hundred yards. Bring your rain gear between April and June; the fall's overspray drenches all who come near.

Other park waterfalls are not as tall, but they're still show-stoppers. An easy walk to 620-foot Bridalveil Fall takes you to an overlook point below its billowing cascade. A more demanding hike to Vernal and Nevada Falls ascends granite steps to the brink of two voluminous drops on the Merced River. If you're only going to do one hike from Yosemite Valley, this should be it. The 7-mile round-trip on the Mist Trail is strenuous, with dozens of tall stone stairs to climb and descend, but the rewards are great. The biggest thrill is hiking so close to the waterfalls that you get thoroughly soaked by their spray.

To see Yosemite at its watery best, time your trip carefully. These waterfalls are fed by snowmelt, so they flow with the greatest vigor in spring. About 75 percent of the high country's snowmelt occurs in April, May and June, so that's prime time for waterfall viewing.

At any time of year, a visit to Yosemite Valley requires careful planning. The valley is extremely popular, and its limited lodgings get booked months in advance, especially from April to October. Book in-park lodgings and tours at www.travelyosemite.com. Park campgrounds also fill up; go to https://www.nps.gov/yose/planyourvisit/camp.htm for information.

YOSEMITE NATIONAL PARK

# Glacier Point

***An eye-candy banquet of peaks and precipices awaits at Yosemite's grandest viewpoint***

## Hot Spot Highlights

- Hike into Yosemite's picture-postcard scenery.
- See the giant sequoias at the Mariposa Grove.
- Ski or snowshoe to Glacier Point and spend the night.

**Address**: Glacier Point Road, Yosemite, CA
**Tel.**: (209) 372-0200
**Website**: www.nps.gov/yose

**Best season:**
Year-round (in winter, access only by skiing)

Roads are not plowed in winter

The commanding vista from Glacier Point, a 7,214-foot granite precipice that lurches over Yosemite Valley, takes in the park's most famous granite icons — Half Dome, Clouds Rest, Liberty Cap, Vernal and Nevada falls, and the surrounding High Sierra. For many park visitors, Glacier Point is the single most photo-worthy spot in Yosemite. It's best seen at sunset, when Half Dome blushes pink, but it's drop-dead gorgeous at any time of day.

Getting to Glacier Point takes about an hour by car or bus from Yosemite Valley, or you can earn the view by hiking the strenuous but scenic Four-Mile Trail. In summer, evening ranger talks are held at Glacier Point's outdoor amphitheater, and stargazing and full-moon programs are offered on summer weekend nights. The Geology Hut, a small stone building built in 1924, offers a photo-op view of Half Dome, North Dome and the Merced River canyon. An imposing log cabin houses a gift shop and café, and in winter, this same building is transformed into an overnight ski cabin.

Although many visitors come to Glacier Point just for the view, your best bet is to take a hike. Nearly a dozen trails start at the point or along its access road. Families enjoy the easy Taft Point and Sentinel Dome trails, which begin at the same parking lot but head in opposite directions. Sentinel Dome, a granite dome at 8,122 feet, offers a breathtaking perspective on Yosemite Falls, and that's only one part of its 360-degree panorama. Taft Point's view is completely different — a head-on look at El Capitan and a stomach-churning view of the Yosemite Valley floor, 3,500 feet below. Hold on to the railing (and your kids!) while you peer over the edge.

For a spectacular one-way hike, follow the Panorama Trail from Glacier Point for 8.5 miles to the Yosemite Valley floor. (You'll need to reserve a spot on the Yosemite Valley Lodge tour bus for a ride up to Glacier Point, then walk back down to your starting

→ **At Glacier Point, it's hard to decide which way to look — but this perspective on Yosemite Falls should not be missed.**

point.) The trail switchbacks downhill, accompanied by ever-changing perspectives on Half Dome, Basket Dome, North Dome, Liberty Cap and, in the distance, Vernal and Nevada falls. Cross over to the Mist Trail and you'll visit the brink of both of these majestic waterfalls before descending the granite staircase to Happy Isles in Yosemite Valley.

In the winter, Glacier Point Road is plowed only as far as Yosemite Ski and Snowboard Area. This small ski resort is California's oldest, and it's a great place to teach beginners how to carve downhill turns. Snowshoers and cross-country skiers can stride or glide from the resort on the unplowed section of Glacier Point Road. Ten miles of the road are groomed, and side trails branch off to destinations like view-filled Dewey Point. Staff from Yosemite's Cross-Country Ski School lead guided trips down the road to Glacier Point's overnight ski hut, where guests are treated to a warm fire, hot meals and a comfy bed. (Experienced skiers can reserve a bunk at

**↑ One of the best times to visit Glacier Point is at sunset, when the sun dropping to the west produces an alpenglow in the east, tinting Half Dome rosy orange.**

**→ Full-grown men look small in the humbling shadows of the Mariposa Grove's giant sequoias.**

the hut and ski in without a guide.) Another overnight ski hut is located on the edge of Ostrander Lake; the 10-mile trail to reach it is ungroomed, so it's a more challenging ski in.

A good side-trip from Glacier Point is the Mariposa Grove of Giant Sequoias. Of Yosemite's three sequoia groves, this is the largest, with more than 500 mature trees, each more than 10 feet in diameter. Casual visitors can stroll through the lower grove to see the most famous "named" trees, like the Grizzly Giant, the grove's largest tree at 210 feet tall and 31 feet across at its base. Adventurous hikers will want to wander around both the upper and lower groves (6 miles round-trip, with a 1,200-foot elevation gain).

# Sequoia and Kings Canyon National Parks

***Adjacent national parks celebrate the largest trees on earth, the United States' deepest canyon and the highest point in the lower 48 states***

### Hot Spot Highlights

- See the chart-topping, mind-boggling General Sherman Tree — the largest on earth by volume.
- Walk the Congress Trail past some of the world's most spectacular giant sequoias.
- Make a heart-pumping climb up 390 stairs to the top of 6,725-foot Moro Rock.
- Enjoy a 31-mile stretch of eye-candy scenery as you drive along the Kings River.
- Hike to a waterfall in a glacial-cut valley.

**Address**: 7050 Generals Hwy, Three Rivers, CA
**Tel.**: (559) 565-3341
**Website**: www.nps.gov/seki

**Best season:**
May to October

Kings Canyon Byway is not plowed in winter

These two side-by-side national parks are famous for their giant sequoias, soaring mountains, deep canyons and roaring rivers. Established in 1890, Sequoia was California's first national park and the United States' second (after Yellowstone). Kings Canyon was designated as a national park much later, in 1940. Now managed jointly by the National Park Service, these two parks abound with superlatives. Within their borders are Mount Whitney, the highest point in the contiguous United States at 14,495 feet, and the Kings River Canyon, one of the deepest canyons in the world. Even so, the parks are most revered for their super-sized sequoias — the General Sherman, the world's largest tree by volume, and its gargantuan neighbors.

→ **Wander along the Congress Trail to feel the awe of giant sequoias. These gargantuan trees have been growing since before King Arthur's knights gathered at the Round Table.**

↘ **Occasionally a giant sequoia will fall for no apparent reason except that it has reached the end of its lifespan, which could be 20 centuries or more. This one toppled on a calm, windless summer day.**

↙ **Black bears are common throughout the Sierra Nevada and are generally not aggressive toward humans, although they will occasionally break into buildings and cars for food.**

## Giant Forest

Giant Forest has the most impressive collection of giant sequoias of anywhere in Sequoia and Kings Canyon National Park. Among its 8,000 giant sequoias is the General Sherman, a 2,100-year-old tree that's the largest living thing on earth by volume. Other trees are taller or wider, but none has the combined height and width of this leviathan. This giant sequoia is 275 feet tall — taller than a 27-story building — and still growing. Every year it adds enough wood to make another 60-foot-tall tree. At the ground, its circumference is 102.6 feet. One branch of the General Sherman is so big — almost 7 feet in diameter — that it's larger than most trees east of the Mississippi.

Not surprisingly, the General Sherman attracts a crowd, which is why the park runs shuttle buses to two separate stops, one above and one below this amazing tree.

↑ **The General Sherman tree draws a crowd, and rightfully so. In terms of sheer bulk, it's the largest living thing on earth.**

Many visitors get off at the upper stop and walk one-way downhill to the lower stop, passing the General Sherman along the way. That's fine for a quick trip, but you can get an even bigger dose of sequoia awesomeness by hiking the adjacent Congress Trail, a 2.1-mile loop that travels through dozens of sequoias with diameters the size of your living room. The House and Senate groves, two massive sequoia clusters near the trail's end, are the most impressive, but another standout is the Washington Tree, which was long considered the world's second-largest tree. It used to be just 20 feet shorter than the General Sherman, but after a lightning fire burned its upper reaches in the late 1990s, it no longer makes the top 30. (Park at the General Sherman Tree parking lot off Wolverton Road, then walk downhill to the tree, or take the free shuttle bus.)

Continue your Giant Forest visit at the Giant Forest Museum, which is housed in a renovated 1928 building. Originally a market, the building now serves as museum, visitor center and bookstore, plus the hub for many Giant Forest trails. Several paths are suitable for wheelchairs, including the Big Trees Trail and the General Sherman Tree Trail. In addition to spending time in the humbling shadows of the sequoias, don't miss visiting lovely Crescent Meadow. A short walk around the meadow's circumference will lead you to Tharp's Log, the summer abode of rancher Hale Tharp. The first white man to enter Giant Forest, Tharp built his home inside a hollowed, fire-scarred sequoia log and lived in it for nearly 30 summers from 1861 to 1890. You can still see his simple dining room table and the door and window frames he built into the log. On the road to Crescent Meadow is another tree curiosity — the Tunnel Log, a fallen sequoia that was tunneled out so that cars could drive through. It's a popular spot for photos.

Near Crescent Meadow is Moro Rock, a 6,725-foot bald granite dome that protrudes from a forested ridge and is accessed via a series of staircases and ramps. You make your way up 390 stairs, holding tight to railings that line the rock-blasted trail. To catch your breath, stop to admire the view of the Kaweah River gorge far below, or the zig-zagging switchbacks of the Generals Highway as it heads south toward Three Rivers. Once you've gained Moro Rock's flat summit, lean on the iron railing and admire the view of the Great Western Divide, a saw-toothed skyline of alpine cirques and glacier-carved peaks. Landmarks include Castle Rocks, Triple Divide Peak and Mount Stewart. To the west, you can see all the way to the Coast Range, 100 miles away. In closer focus is the Middle Fork of the Kaweah River, 4,000 feet below. But there's one summit you can't see from here, and it's the biggest of them all. Mount Whitney is almost due east from Moro Rock and only about 60 miles away,

**↑ The short hike to the top of Moro Rock is a gym-style stairclimber made by nature. The bald granite dome rewards visitors with views of the Great Western Divide (go early in the morning for the clearest vista).**

↑ **Sierra blazing star delivers a tinge of gold to Kings Canyon's austere granite.**

↗ **There aren't many places in the world where you can drive under a toppled tree, but this massive giant sequoia in Giant Forest makes it possible.**

but because the peaks of the Great Western Divide reach altitudes of 12,000 feet or higher, you can't see over them.

A handful of lodgings and restaurants are found near Giant Forest, including the large and modern Wuksachi Lodge. Farther north in Grant Grove, the John Muir Lodge is a comfortable option. The parks also have campgrounds with sites that can be reserved in advance. For summer reservations, book early.

## Kings Canyon Scenic Byway

There's an undeniable allure about a place called Road's End. That enticing moniker designates the eastern terminus of Highway 180, the Kings Canyon Scenic Byway. Its snaking, winding pavement reaches an end 6 miles past Cedar Grove Village, where the wilderness begins. If you want to continue farther into Kings Canyon, you have to walk.

The drive to reach Road's End is half the fun: from Grant

↑ **Although the majority of visitors come to Sequoia and Kings Canyon in summer, the snowy winter months offer their own inimitable charms.**

Grove, the Kings Canyon Scenic Byway zigzags east for 31 miles, skirting the banks of the roaring Kings River. You'll need to stop often for photo ops, especially in the early season when snowmelt turns the river into a tumbling sea of whitewater. There's a lot to photograph: pullouts along the highway offer overlooks into Kings Canyon, one of the deepest canyons in the world, a stunning 8,200 feet from top to bottom at its highest and lowest points. Be sure to pause at Junction View, where it's easy to picture the relentless force of the Kings River chiseling away at the canyon walls over eons of time. Consider a stop at Boyden Cavern, tucked into tall gray marble cliffs, where you can take a 45-minute tour of its stalactites, speleothems and crystalline helictites. In spring and early summer, Grizzly Falls is worth a look. The 80-foot waterfall

swells with snowmelt as it tumbles off a granite cliff.

Once you arrive at Cedar Grove Village, you'll find a few visitor services: a handful of campgrounds, the 21-room Cedar Grove Lodge, a ranger station and a burger-flipping café. But hiking trails abound: continue another few miles toward Road's End to hike the Zumwalt Meadow Trail, a 1.5-mile self-guided loop

that offers views of imposing granite cliffs carved by glacial action. At the edge of fern-filled Zumwalt Meadow lie clear river pools and a fragrant forest of incense cedars and pines. Or take the 5-minute stroll to Roaring River Falls, a boisterous cascade that makes a powerful noise as it funnels through a narrow gorge. More ambitious hikers follow the Mist Falls Trail, which leads from Road's End to billowing Mist Falls on the South Fork Kings River (8.8 miles round-trip). No matter what path you take, save some time for the best Road's End pastime — sitting by the free-flowing Kings River and watching the water roll by.

**↑ Tokopah Falls in Sequoia National Park makes a great summer hike, and in the winter, you can make the trip on snowshoes.**

**↖ Kings Canyon has dozens of trails for hiking and backpacking, but one of the best ways to spend a day is to sit at Road's End and watch the river roll by.**

**← Mitchell Peak is just one of many summits begging to be climbed in Kings Canyon and Sequoia National Parks.**

SEQUOIA NATIONAL PARK

# Mineral King Valley

***This high-alpine valley carved by glaciers is a gateway to azure lakes, flower-filled meadows and jagged peaks***

### Hot Spot Highlights

- Drive a circuitous mountain road to a hidden alpine valley.
- Hike and camp in a subalpine wonderland bisected by the East Fork Kaweah River.
- See historic cabins and silver-mining sites.

**Address**: Mineral King Ranger Station, Mile 24, Mineral King Road, Three Rivers, CA
**Tel.**: (559) 565-3768 or (559) 565-3341
**Website**: www.nps.gov/seki/planyourvisit/mkdayhikesum.htm

**Best season:**
June to October

Roads are not plowed in winter

**↗ The Mineral King Ranger Station should be your first stop for maps and updates on trail conditions.**

In Sequoia National Park's remote southern reaches, the distinctly pointed pinnacle of Sawtooth Peak towers over Mineral King Valley, a 7,400-foot glacial bowl framed by 11,000-foot summits and wildflower meadows. This hikers' and backpackers' paradise has a fascinating and somewhat contentious history, starting with an 1872 silver-mining boom that led to the construction of 36 mills and a town. Within a decade, the boom went bust, and the get-rich-quick schemers departed. Nearly a century later, filmmaker and entrepreneur Walt Disney tried to commercialize Mineral King Valley by turning it into a 27-lift ski resort. Preservationists fought Disney's plan, but it was Mother Nature that dealt the final blow: in the winter of 1969, a massive avalanche wiped out several buildings on Disney's property. He gave up his dream.

Today Mineral King Valley offers no promise of riches, save for its wealth of alpine lakes and meadows, a vertical banquet of granite and shale mountains, and the headwaters of the East Fork of the Kaweah

↑ **Mineral King's rockbound lakes are classic glacial tarns, their basins deeply scoured by advancing ice floes.**

River. For nature lovers, that's more than enough.

Start with a mellow walk along Cold Springs Campground's nature trail, which follows the banks of the East Fork Kaweah River. Riverfront views of the Sawtooth Ridge are glorious, especially at sunset when the mountain peaks reflect the pinks and corals of the setting sun. Interpretive signs identify junipers, red and white firs, cottonwoods, and aspens. From the far end of the loop, you can continue another half mile to Mineral King Valley, then retrace your steps.

A more ambitious trek begins at the Sawtooth Trailhead and climbs 2,500 feet to the rocky, gemlike Monarch Lakes. The first mile to Groundhog Meadow is remarkably steep, but then the grade mellows. The last mile is chiseled out of colorful cliffs; only a few stalwart western junipers grow in an austere landscape of rusty red shale, white marble, gray granite, and black metamorphic slate. Snow is often found near the lake, even in late summer. From Lower Monarch Lake,

**↑ Upper Monarch Lake is an alpine infinity pool, its cobalt waters spilling over a granite ledge and cascading downhill to Mineral King Valley.**

**→ Near the base of White Chief Peak, tiny alpine wildflowers bloom as late as August.**

the main trail continues northward to Sawtooth Pass, but a hiker-made trail leads southeast for 0.5 mile to Upper Monarch Lake. It's worth the climb, if only to look back down on the lower lake from above.

The 3.4-mile Eagle Lake Trail follows the same route as the Mosquito Lakes Trail until the 2-mile point, where it veers left for Eagle Lake and ascends another 1,000 feet over 1.4 miles. Much of the climb travels over an exposed boulder field, but well-graded switchbacks make the climb easier. The big lake is dotted with a few rocky islands and framed by glacially carved rock. Brook trout swim in crystal-clear waters. The trail continues along the lake's west side to picnicking spots and photo opportunities.

From the same trailhead, the White Chief Mine hike is a great trip for history fans and wildflower aficionados. White Chief Trail departs from the Mosquito/Eagle Lakes trail after the first mile and climbs steeply until it tops out at a high meadow, where some of Mineral King's tallest peaks pop into view. Next comes White Chief Meadows, surrounded by high granite walls and filled with dozens of downed trees — evidence of harsh winter avalanches. Foxtail pines, one of the rarer species of Sierra conifers, grow in this area. Beyond the meadow, the trail ascends slightly until it nears a waterfall on White Chief Creek. In mid- to late summer, this area hosts an explosion of tiny alpine wildflowers. Look for the opening to White Chief Mine in a band of white marble just above the trail. The tunnel dead-ends in about 150 feet, but its yawning mouth makes for a good photo spot.

While you hike, you're sure to see yellow-bellied marmots, those cute and furry members of the squirrel family that are common throughout the Sierra Nevada's higher elevations. In Mineral King, the "whistle pig" (so named for its shrill cry) is something of a menace. No one is sure exactly why, but in May and June, marmots sometimes crawl into car engines and

chew on rubber radiator hoses and plastic wiring. Visitors — especially backpackers who leave their cars parked for extended periods — have had their vehicles disabled by hungry marmots. To discourage the critters, Mineral King cabin owners wrap the undersides of their cars with tarps, blocking the marmots' access to engine compartments. Late-summer visitors need not be concerned because by mid-July the marmots' food cravings change, and they lose interest in cars.

Driving to Mineral King is a challenge and a commitment, thanks to its narrow and circuitous access road. Mineral King Road is open from Memorial Day weekend through October (possibly longer if it doesn't snow). It's a 25-mile drive from the small town of Three Rivers, with a whopping 698 curves and turns. It takes at least an hour to cover these 25 miles, and once you arrive, plan to spend at least a couple of days before making the return trip on that same daunting road. Silver City Resort is open to the public and offers cabins for rent, a café and a small general store. The resort, two campgrounds (Cold Springs and Atwell Mill) and a small ranger station are the only visitor services in Mineral King. The nearest gas station is in the town of Three Rivers, so make sure your tank is filled up.

↑ From almost everywhere in Mineral King Valley, you can see the jagged outline of Sawtooth Peak.

← Endemic to California, robust foxtail pines live for more than a century in the high reaches of Mineral King Valley.

→ The yellow-bellied marmot is one of the most social members of the squirrel family. It has few predators and will often whistle as you walk past.

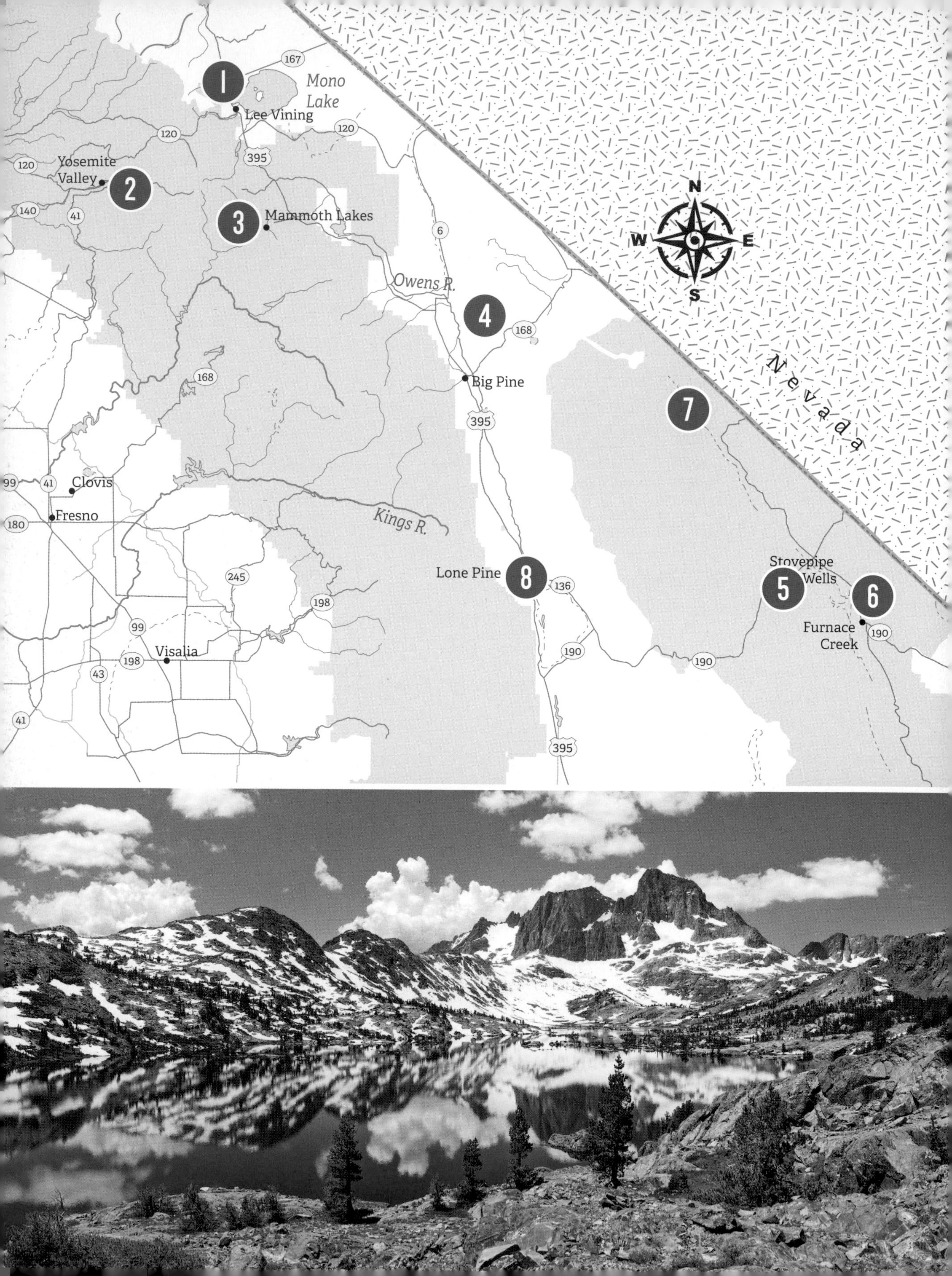

Mono Lake
Lee Vining
Yosemite Valley
Mammoth Lakes
Owens R.
Big Pine
Nevada
N
W
E
S
Clovis
Fresno
Kings R.
Lone Pine
Stovepipe Wells
Furnace Creek
Visalia
167
120
395
140
41
6
168
99
180
245
198
136
190
43
1
2
3
4
5
6
7
8

# Eastern Sierra Nevada and Death Valley

# Mono Lake

***An ancient saline lake provides a haven for migratory birds***

## Hot Spot Highlights

- Witness an exceptional gathering of resident and migratory birds.
- See brine shrimp swimming in alkaline waters.
- Walk or canoe among the tufa towers.

**Address**: Mono Basin Scenic Area and Visitor Center, 1 Visitor Center Drive, Hwy 395, Lee Vining, CA
**Tel.**: (760) 647-3044
**Websites**:
www.fs.usda.gov/recarea/inyo/recarea/?recid=20252, www.parks.ca.gov/?page_id=514, www.monolake.org

**Best season:**
Year-round

**↗ Phalaropes — both Wilson's and red-necked — are sophisticated feeders that can paddle in circles with specially adapted feet to draw brine shrimp to the surface.**

Framed by the Sierra mountains to the west and desert to the east, Mono Lake lures legions of photographers, birdwatchers and scenery-seekers who want to see "one of the strangest freaks of nature to be found in any land" — as described by American writer Mark Twain in 1863. A majestic body of water covering about 60 square miles, Mono Lake is three times saltier than the ocean and 80 times as alkaline. Go for a swim in Mono Lake, and you'll find yourself nearly buoyant.

Located near the town of Lee Vining, just east of Yosemite National Park, the ancient lake has no natural outlet, only inlet streams. During the course of its 800,000-year life — it's one of the oldest lakes in North America — salts and minerals washed into its waters, creating an unusual chemistry experiment. Underwater springs containing calcium combined with the saline water to create tufa formations — tall, off-white, coral-like structures that line the lakeshore and poke up from the lake's shallow edges.

The tufa formations grow upright, swelling into odd vertical shapes as spring water pushes upward inside them. The tufas only stop growing when exposed to air, which disrupts the chemical reaction.

Two standout features of Mono Lake are its huge, bald islands, Paoha and Negit. These cinder-cone islands have figured prominently in the lake's preservation. Starting in 1941, four streams that fed Mono Lake were diverted into the California Aqueduct to provide water for Los Angeles. The lake began to shrink rapidly, losing an average of 18 inches per year. As the water level dropped, a land bridge formed. Coyotes were able to access Paoha and Negit, and they devastated

the bird populations. After a long conservation battle and much legal wrangling, laws were passed that gave California's Water Resources Board the authority to regulate Mono Lake's water level so that its natural resources are protected. Since this regulation, the lake level has risen substantially, and it will continue to rise over the coming decades. Today, Mono Lake is viewed as one of California's great environmental victories.

The lake is a godsend for birds — millions of them — who use it as a migration stop as they pass over the desert lands to the east. To feathered creatures, Mono Lake's biggest attraction is its population of half-inch-long brine shrimp. From April to October, thick masses of these tiny shrimp cluster near the lake surface, creating an all-you-can-eat buffet for birds. During the peak of summer, about 10 to 12 trillion brine shrimp live in the lake's waters. Additionally, millions of alkali flies buzz along the shoreline, providing additional bird food.

Peak birding season is summer and fall, but interesting species can be seen in any month of the year. More than 80 types of migratory birds depend on Mono Lake for food and a rest stop on their long journeys. In August, the amazing Wilson's phalarope fattens up here, then makes a 3,000-mile nonstop flight to South America in a mere 3 days. In September and October, the showstopper species is the

**↑ Underwater springs containing calcium carbonate have combined with Mono Lake's saline and alkaline water to create massive tufa formations.**

**↓ If you see a California gull anywhere along the Pacific coast, chances are good it was born at Mono Lake.**

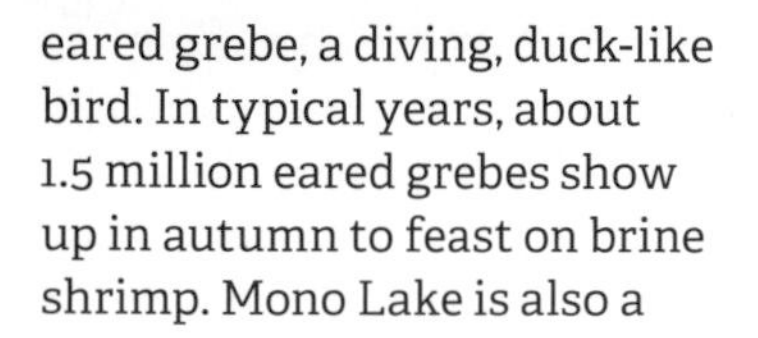

eared grebe, a diving, duck-like bird. In typical years, about 1.5 million eared grebes show up in autumn to feast on brine shrimp. Mono Lake is also a huge breeding area for California gulls — more than 80 percent of the gulls that live on the California coast are born here.

Near the town of Lee Vining, there are several access points for the lake. Start your trip at the Mono Basin Scenic Area Visitor Center, perched high on a hill above the lake, where exhibits detail Mono Lake's geologic and human history. A 1.5-mile trail leads from the visitor center to the Old Marina site, where you can see several large tufa towers. To get a more in-depth look, take a walk on the short trail at Mono Lake Tufa State Natural Reserve, which travels along

boardwalks to the lakeshore and passes by dozens of tufa towers. Photographers are attracted to this area for its surreal tufa landscape, ecological wonders and Technicolor sunsets and sunrises.

Birders should head straight to Mono Lake County Park, 2 miles north of Lee Vining off Cemetery Road. A boardwalk trail leads through the willows and marsh to the lake's edge, and an overlook platform offers views of shorebirds feeding and ospreys tending to their nests on top of tufa towers. The county park also has a nice picnic area with shady cottonwood trees, drinking water, picnic tables and restrooms.

If you're visiting on a summer weekend, don't miss taking a guided canoe tour with the Mono Lake Committee, the nonprofit organization that has fought to preserve Mono Lake since 1978. Reserve your spot in advance (www.monolake.org).

From May to October, the small town of Lee Vining offers a dozen motels, a handful of restaurants and a grocery store. In winter and early spring, many businesses are closed, so plan accordingly.

**↑ Mono Lake's tufa towers host nesting ospreys and the world's largest tufa-nesting colony of violet-green swallows, who make their homes in the tufa's nooks and crannies.**

**↖ One of the best ways to see Mono Lake's otherworldly tufa formations is to take a canoe tour with the Mono Lake Committee.**

**← In early autumn, the very social eared grebe gathers on Mono Lake's surface in massive flocks totaling more than a million individuals.**

# John Muir Trail

***A jewel in the crown of America's long-distance hiking trails***

## Hot Spot Highlights

- Hike one of America's most scenic long-distance trails.
- Climb up and over six mountain passes higher than 11,000 feet.
- Summit the highest peak in the contiguous United States — 14,505-foot Mount Whitney.

**Address**: The trail begins at Happy Isles in Yosemite Valley and ends at the Whitney Portal Trailhead in Lone Pine, CA
**Tel.**: Pacific Crest Trail Association: (916) 285-1846
**Website**: www.pcta.org/discover-the-trail/john-muir-trail/

**Best season:**
July to September

**↗ The enticingly aromatic leopard lily is one of the Sierra's most coveted flowers. Look for them in moist seeps between 8,000 and 9,000 feet.**

**↗↗ A common high-alpine flower, pussy paws has the ability to thermoregulate. In cool temperatures, it lays flat on the ground, but as the day heats up, its stems lift off the warm soil.**

The John Muir Trail, a 211-mile path stretching from Yosemite Valley to Mount Whitney — the highest peak in the contiguous United States — is a bucket-list trip for seasoned trekkers and backpackers. Named in honor of conservationist and author John Muir, whose writing led to the protection of much of the West's wildlands, the long-distance trail offers sublime panoramas of deep sapphire lakes, granite cliffs and spires, and high-alpine vistas.

Most backpackers complete the John Muir Trail in about 3 weeks, covering 10 to 15 miles per day with occasional layover days. But it's possible to do it much faster — in 2017, a French ultrarunner set an astonishing speed record of less than 3 days.

A few of the trail's highlights include the glaciated granite domes of Tuolumne Meadows, the volcanic landscape near Devils Postpile, the lakes of Evolution Valley and the astonishing vista from the 14,505-foot summit of Mount Whitney. But for most hikers, it's the austere high passes they remember best, mostly because of the extreme effort required to cross them. The trail follows the High Sierra's spine, climbing up and over 10 mountain passes, including 6 that are higher than 11,000 feet (Donahue, Muir, Mather, Pinchot, Glen and Forester). Donahue Pass, at 11,056 feet, leads from Yosemite downhill into the Ansel Adams Wilderness and a few of the Sierra's most photographed destinations — Banner Peak,

↑ The John Muir Trail's sublime scenery makes hikers forget their heavy backpacks and tired feet.

→ Evolution Basin invites hikers to linger with its cascading waterfalls, deep lakes and banquet of granite peaks.

Thousand Island Lake and Garnet Lake. Muir Pass, at 11,995 feet, is set in a stark landscape of glacial rock and icy blue lakes. It's crowned by the octagon-shaped Muir Hut, a rock shelter built more than a century ago by the Sierra Club to honor John Muir. Even higher and more arduous is Forester Pass, at 13,200 feet, often covered in ice and snow even late in the summer. Much of this glacially sculpted land-scape will remind you of Ansel

Adams' photographs — he did much of his most famous work in this part of the Sierra.

Hiking the John Muir Trail is an arduous adventure and requires substantial advance planning. About 165 miles of the trail overlaps with the world-famous Pacific Crest Trail, which spans 2,650 miles from Mexico to Canada, and both trails are popular with hikers from all over the world. Hiking permits must be reserved far in advance. The season is very short — typically the trail is snow-free by mid-July and the weather stays good until late September. It's nearly impossible to carry 3 weeks' worth of food, so hikers must arrange to resupply at various points along the trail. Some choose to utilize pack stock (mule trains) to carry in resupplies. But with solid planning (and proper training for hiking at high altitude), this trek is a worthy lifetime achievement.

**↑ One of the Sierra's most iconic images is 12,942-foot Banner Peak, its glaciers appearing like white frosting, framing Garnet Lake.**

**← Even as late as July, hikers find themselves crossing thick snowfields at high points along the trail.**

# Devils Postpile National Monument

***The San Joaquin River flows past a massive pile of hexagonal volcanic posts, then plummets over rock as a misty waterfall***

### Hot Spot Highlights

- See one of the world's finest examples of columnar basalt.
- Hike to a breathtaking river waterfall.
- Fly-fish the Middle Fork San Joaquin River.

**Address**: Shuttle bus departs from 10001 Minaret Road, Mammoth Lakes, CA
**Tel.**: (760) 934-2289
**Website**: www.nps.gov/depo

**Best season:**
June to October

→ **At the base of the Devils Postpile lies the chaotic rubble of fallen lava columns, their sharp hexagonal shapes still intact.**

Few U.S. national parks are designated with monikers as intriguing as Devils Postpile National Monument. The name refers to a collection of basalt columns remaining from an ancient lava flow. The 60-foot-high "pile" looks something like a vertical stack of candles. Most are perfectly straight and upright, but others curve like they've been left out in the sun. At the base of the pile is a heap of rubble — the crumbled remains of collapsed posts.

This formation of basalt rock columns is visual proof that the Mammoth Lakes area is volcanic country. The town sits on the Long Valley Caldera, one of Earth's largest calderas — and potentially one of the most active. About 80,000 years ago, lava filled the San Joaquin Valley more than 400 feet deep. As the lava began to cool from the air flow on top, it also cooled simultaneously from the hard granite bedrock below. This caused the lava to harden and crack into tall, narrow pieces, forming nearly perfect columns or posts. Although there are other lava columns found throughout the world (the closest example is at Columns of the Giants in Sonora Pass, north of Yosemite), the Devils Postpile is considered to be the globe's finest example. The columns here are more regular in size and shape, and more distinctively hexagonal than anywhere else. The curvature in some of the columns was caused by the varying rates at which the massive lava flow cooled.

Unless you have camping reservations or a handicap placard or license plates, you must ride a shuttle bus into the monument during the peak season, June to early September. The shuttle departs from the Mammoth Mountain Ski Area gondola building and drops passengers near the Devils Postpile Ranger Station, where the Middle Fork of the San Joaquin River flows

↑ **A climb to the top of the Devils Postpile reveals the remarkable symmetry of the hexagonal lava columns, their tops polished by glaciers.**

↗ **On warm summer days, walk to the base of Rainbow Falls to enjoy the coolness of its misty spray.**

→ **Rainbow Falls pours over a rhyodacite cliff on the Middle Fork San Joaquin River. See its namesake rainbow at midday, when the sun is highest.**

past. This is one of the Sierras' top fly-fishing streams, filled with rainbow, brown, brook, and even some golden trout.

From the station, walk an easy third of a mile downriver through meadows and fir forests to the base of the Postpile. The wow factor from this vantage point is enough to make the trip worthwhile, but the formation seems even more surreal from on top. Under your feet, the columns' edges look like honeycomb or tiles that have been laid side by side. About 65,000 years after lava formed these columns, the glaciers moved across them and shined their tops with a glacial polish.

A trip to Devils Postpile National Monument isn't complete without a visit to Rainbow Falls, a 1.5-mile hike from the Postpile. This is one of the Sierras' most dramatic and photogenic river waterfalls. It plummets 101 feet over a cliff of rhyodacite — a different type of volcanic rock than the basalt that makes up the Postpile. The rhyodacite forms an extremely hard horizontal layer at the waterfall's lip, which keeps the river from eroding the waterfall and eventually beveling it off. True to its name, Rainbow Falls has a rainbow that dances through the mist near its base. The rainbow is best seen at midday, when direct light rays pass through the spraying water droplets.

If you want to spend the

night in this beautiful monument, Red's Meadow Lodge offers rustic housekeeping cabins and motel rooms, and six campgrounds are open in summer: Agnew Meadow, Pumice, Upper Soda Springs, Minaret Falls, Red's Meadow, and Devils Postpile. A wide variety of motels, resorts and condos is available in the town of Mammoth Lakes.

# Ancient Bristlecone Pine Forest

***The arid White Mountains are home to the oldest trees in the world, some living for more than 45 centuries***

## Hot Spot Highlights

- Walk among the oldest trees in the world.
- See the world's largest bristlecone pine.
- Hike to the summit of California's third-highest peak.

**Address**: Schulman Grove Visitor Center, State Route 168 by Westgard Pass, 24 miles from Big Pine, CA
**Tel.**: (442) 228-5002 or (760) 873-2501
**Website**: https://esiaonline.org/new-page-1

**Best season:**
May to October

❶ Roads may not be plowed in winter

In the alpine desert east of Big Pine, ancient bristlecone pines — photogenic icons with twisted trunks, contorted limbs and bushy needles — punctuate the lofty reaches of the White-Inyo Mountains, an arid range that parallels the wetter Sierra Nevada. Gnarled specimens of Great Basin bristlecone pines cling to the alkaline soils of 10,000-foot slopes, a harsh living situation that causes them to grow very slowly. Some were seedlings at the time when the Egyptian pyramids were being built.

The bristlecone pine's rot-resistant and resin-rich wood can last for millennia, but to the naked eye, some trees look more like sculpted driftwood than thriving flora. Their beautifully wind-scoured trunks and gnarled limbs may be comprised of mostly dead wood, but a thin ribbon of life runs through their branches.

At the Schulman Grove Visitor Center, walk among the ancient trees on the 4.3-mile Methuselah Trail. The 4,850-year-old Methuselah was considered to be the oldest documented living tree in the world until 2013, when scientists discovered an even older tree (more than 5,000 years old) growing in the same grove. These two ancients lie approximately halfway around the loop, but the trees are not marked or labeled in any way to protect them from being trampled. No matter — it's satisfying just knowing you have walked among the ancients. The path follows a meandering route through both old and young bristlecones, plus a few limber and piñon pines. The ground beneath the pines is marked with angular outcrops of white dolomite, a highly alkaline limestone.

The 1-mile Discovery Trail loop also begins at the visitor center. Interpretive signs describe the work of Dr. Edmund Schulman, the scientist who is credited with "discovering" these ancient trees. In the mid-1950s, Schulman was an early pioneer in the science of dendrochronology, or tree growth-ring dating. Although many Native Americans and early white settlers

knew about the bristlecones, Schulman was the first to count their rings and note their outstanding longevity.

Twelve miles beyond the visitor center lies the Patriarch Grove, home to the Patriarch Tree, the world's largest bristlecone pine (36 feet in circumference). A short hiking trail leads to it. Four miles farther is a high-altitude research station and the trail to the summit of White Mountain, the third-highest summit in California at 14,246 feet. An old military road climbs 2,600 feet to the summit (a 15-mile round-trip). The impressive granite massif offers grand views — to the east, extending 200 miles into Nevada, and to the west, the Owens Valley and Volcanic Tableland, plus a wide panorama of the Sierra Nevada. Some hikers pack along their headlamps to do all or part of the trip by moonlight.

The drive to the Schulman Grove Visitor Center is slow going, with a 6,000-foot ascent from Big Pine and no gas stations or stores along the route. Plan on an hour for the 23-mile drive from town, and bring a picnic and several bottles of water — you'll need it for the dry air at 10,000 feet (there's no water at the trailhead or visitor center).

**↑ The bristlecone pine produces male and female cones on the same tree. These female cones have sharp, hooked spines that give rise to the tree's name.**

**↖ Ancient bristlecone pines often look more like gnarled driftwood than living trees, and they thrive in some of the earth's harshest conditions — alkaline dolomite soils, high winds and months of bitterly cold temperatures.**

DEATH VALLEY NATIONAL PARK

# Stovepipe Wells

***Miles of sand dunes, a polished marble canyon and a remarkable fish can be found in Death Valley's central region***

### Hot Spot Highlights

- Climb sand dunes at sunrise or sunset to see ever-changing colors and shadows.
- See the endangered desert pupfish in a saline creek.
- Hike through a marbleized slickrock canyon.

**Address**: Death Valley National Park; from Lone Pine on U.S. 395, drive east on Hwy 136 for 18 miles then continue east on Hwy 190 for approximately 60 miles to Stovepipe Wells Village
**Tel.**: (760) 786-3200
**Websites**: www.nps.gov/deva, www.dvnha.org

**Best season:**
October to April

Dangerously hot in summer months

**↗ The Mosaic Canyon hike begins at the gaping canyon mouth, then squeezes into a narrow slick-rock chute, then twists and turns until it opens out to a higher wash.**

For visitors entering Death Valley from the west, Stovepipe Wells is the first major stopping point after a long and twisty drive through the desert hills. Originally settled as a mining outpost in the early 1900s, this tiny hamlet is now a welcoming place for park travelers. A privately operated motel, campground, general store, saloon and restaurant are found here; reserve at www.deathvalleyhotels.com.

## Mosaic Canyon

The marbled narrows of Mosaic Canyon are a geologist's art museum, a place to walk slowly and look closely, as you would in the Louvre. Dolomite, transformed into marble by heat and pressure, then polished by water, has created colorful swirls in the bedrock. Eons of time and countless flash floods have embedded the smooth canyon walls with mosaic breccia, multicolored rock fragments that appear to be cemented together. An easy stroll through the canyon's lower reaches shows off colorful slickrock and shiny marble. As you progress up the canyon, the walls close in tighter around you. At just past the

↑ **The colorful walls of Mosaic Canyon were formed, exposed and polished by countless flash floods over eons of time.**

half-mile mark, the canyon opens out to a wide alluvial fan. Many visitors turn around here, but intrepid hikers can continue another 1.5 miles until the canyon ends at a dry waterfall, too high to be scaled.

## Mesquite Flat Sand Dunes

For a hike that will delight hikers of all ages and abilities, take a walk in the 90-foot-high Mesquite Flat Sand Dunes. These aren't Death Valley's tallest sand dunes — those are the Eureka Dunes in the park's northern region — but they are the most accessible, located just a short drive from Stovepipe Wells. The dunes have no marked trail because of the continually shifting desert sands, so you must improvise: make a beeline from the parking lot to the highest sandy ridgeline. How far you wander is completely up to you. The best time to visit is just before sunrise or around sunset because of the incredible show of color and light. In the early morning, you can spot animal tracks made by creatures during the night, most often the tiny footprints of birds and rodents. Full-moon nights on the dunes are also spectacular, but nighttime hikers should watch for nocturnal rattlesnakes.

## Salt Creek

Death Valley's arid, desolate landscape was once part of a massive freshwater lake, and a surviving remnant of that lake is found at Salt Creek. The waterway is home to the Salt Creek pupfish, a 2-inch-long fish that lives nowhere else in the world. This is a highly resourceful fish: when the giant lake dried up about 10,000 years ago, its fresh water slowly converted to salt water, and the amazing pupfish evolved to survive in its salty new environment. The pupfish also has the ability to survive in water from near-freezing temperatures to almost 108 degrees Fahrenheit — and it occasionally experiences both extremes. From the trailhead, a wheelchair-accessible boardwalk crosses a wetland of saltgrass and pickleweed, tracing along Salt Creek's path. In February and March, peer down into the pools, and you may spot the minnow-sized pupfish swimming. In the heat of summer, the fish go dormant. But at any time of year, songbirds and great blue herons congregate, and the stream's salty pools reflect the blue sky and surrounding badlands.

**↑ A wooden boardwalk travels alongside Salt Creek, a saline wetland that harbors the remarkably well-adapted Salt Creek pupfish.**

**← Continually shifting sands create a Sahara-like expanse of dunes at Mesquite Flat, where photographers gather at dawn and dusk to capture vivid pinks and golds.**

DEATH VALLEY NATIONAL PARK

# Furnace Creek

***The hottest, driest and lowest place in North America***

## Hot Spot Highlights

- Explore America's hottest and driest place.
- Walk in the Western Hemisphere's lowest spot.
- Catch an amazing spring wildflower show.
- Photograph multicolored badlands.

**Address**: Death Valley National Park; from Lone Pine on U.S. 395, drive east on Hwy 136 for 18 miles then continue east on Hwy 190 for approximately 80 miles to the Furnace Creek Visitor Center
**Tel.**: (760) 786-3200
**Websites**: www.nps.gov/deva, www.dvnha.org

**Best season:**
October to April

❶ Dangerously hot in summer months

**↗ In peak flower years, the sunflower known as desert gold rolls out a stunning carpet on Death Valley's floor. By blooming en masse, the flower can attract greater numbers of pollinators.**

The largest U.S. national park outside of Alaska, Death Valley's 5,000 square miles and 3.3 million acres encompass soaring sand dunes, below-sea-level salt flats and colorful sandstone canyons. Here, extremes are the norm: Death Valley is America's hottest and driest place, with summer temperatures peaking above 120 degrees Fahrenheit, and rainfall averaging less than 2 inches per year. Also extreme are the park's high and low elevations — the salt flats at Badwater Basin rest at 282 feet below sea level, while Telescope Peak soars to 11,049 feet.

First-time visitors are astonished by Death Valley's vast spaces. Allow plenty of time for driving from one destination to the next. For short stays of only a day or two, maximize your exploring (and minimize your driving time) by sticking to the park's central region near Stovepipe Wells and Furnace Creek. If you have additional days, add on trips to the park's northern region (see pages 172–75).

In good rain years, blossoms

↑ **A hike up the colorful badlands of Golden Canyon reveals sculpted rock layers tinted by mineral deposits from an ancient Ice Age lake.**

push up from the sand as early as Valentine's Day near Furnace Creek and Badwater Basin. Look for fields of desert gold, brown-eyed evening primrose and purple notch-leaved phacelia from your car window along Badwater Road and on Highway 190 near the Furnace Creek Inn. The low-desert regions are also home to the aptly named desert five-spot, with its quintuple crimson spots highlighting lavender petals.

Death Valley encompasses a vast, remote area. Make sure your car is fully loaded with gasoline, snacks and drinking water. Visitor services are few. The National Park Service operates 11 campgrounds throughout the park; all are first-come, first-served except Furnace Creek (reservations available October 15 to April 15 at www.recreation.gov). The Ranch at Death Valley is a privately operated motel and restaurant. If you're willing to splurge, book a stay at the luxurious 1920s Inn at Death Valley. Rooms at both the Ranch and the Inn can be reserved at www.oasisatdeathvalley.com.

↑ **At Zabriskie Point, sharply silhouetted hills are folded and uplifted, their rich mineral content creating a rainbow of rich colors and deeply shadowed crevices.**

## Golden Canyon and Zabriskie Point

Every imaginable shade of gold — from orange to apricot to school-bus yellow — is visible in the wrinkled Golden Canyon cliffs, whose folded and eroded layers glow at sunrise and sunset. Pick your favorite perspective and mode of travel: drive to Zabriskie Point and survey the scene from on high, or see the vibrant beauty up close by hiking in Golden Canyon. For casual sightseers, Zabriskie Point (off Highway 190) offers a stunning view of the multihued badlands from a 100-yard-long paved trail. It's one of the park's most photographed viewpoints and a deservedly busy spot at sunset. The Golden Canyon hike starts from the cliffs' opposite side (off Badwater Road, 3.5 miles south of the visitor center). The 2-mile round-trip trail heads gently uphill through soft canyon walls colorfully banded in yellow, beige and cream, signifying the presence of varied minerals. A highlight near trail's end is Red Cathedral, a towering cliff colored by the weathering of iron-rich sediments. It's also possible to make a 5-mile loop out of this trip by turning right at a junction shortly before Red Cathedral, then hiking through the

↑ **It's hard to imagine a more surreal landscape than the crinkled salt flats of Badwater Basin, the lowest point in the Western Hemisphere.**

colorful badlands of Gower Gulch, along the shoulder of Manly Beacon, and back to the mouth of Golden Canyon. Or, with a car shuttle, you can hike one-way from Golden Canyon to Zabriskie Point.

## Badwater Basin

No trip to Death Valley would be complete without a visit to Badwater Basin, the lowest point in the Western Hemisphere, which tips the altimeter at 282 feet below sea level. Its vast expanse of salt flats and salty puddles were a terrible disappointment to thirsty emigrants who crossed this desert in the 1800s in search of a better life. The salty puddles — which can expand to become a large pond immediately after a big rainstorm — are all that remains of a lake that was more than 600 feet deep a million years ago. In its wake is a surreal tract of sodium chloride, better known as table salt. Walk out as far as you like onto the salt flats, and look back toward the road to note the negative elevation sign on the high cliff.

## Artist's Drive

Just down the road from Badwater Basin is the turnoff for Artist's Drive, a paved road that bypasses the main

↑ **The Artist's Drive is best viewed at the end of the day, when iron, mica and manganese deposits glow in the warm, saturated light.**

highway and shows off the colorful hues of the Amargosa Range's sedimentary hills in its 9-mile stretch. Because traffic is one-way (south to north) on this single-lane road, you can drive at your own pace, taking time to admire the results of millions of years of oxidation in this silent, rainbow-hued canyon. Over the millennia, flash floods have exposed deposits of iron (pink, red and yellow), mica (green), and manganese (purple) to the air. Stop at the pullout parking area for Artist's Palette, where the colors are especially dazzling. If possible, time your visit here for late afternoon, when the artist's multihued palette — pink, mauve, gold, green and lavender — is the most vivid.

## Harmony Borax Works

Borax was first discovered in Death Valley in 1881, but transporting it proved difficult

because the nearest railroad was 165 miles away over rugged desert terrain. Enterprising miners figured out a solution: they built specially designed wagons that could carry huge loads pulled by teams of 20 mules. The rest, as they say, is history. An icon of the Old West, the 20-mule teams of the 1880s hauled heavy loads of borax from Furnace Creek to the Mojave railroad, a grueling 6-day trip. At the Harmony Borax Works site, a wheelchair-accessible loop trail leads past an original 20-mule team wagon and the adobe ruins of the borax works, where the mineral was scraped from the ground, processed and refined. The refinery operated only from 1883 to 1888, but it was prosperous for that short time. At the west end of the loop, leave the trail and walk out to the crusty salt flats, where Chinese laborers scraped borax right off the surface.

**↑ Death Valley's stark hills and bleached mudflats harbor the ruins of borax mining operations that flourished against all odds.**

# Death Valley National Park Northern Region

***Natural oddities appear in an arid landscape: traveling rocks, a volcanic crater and California's tallest sand dunes***

### Hot Spot Highlights

- Marvel at the "moving" rocks that leave tracks in the playa.
- Climb to the top of California's tallest sand dunes.
- Circumnavigate the rim of a 600-foot-deep crater.

**Address**: Death Valley National Park; from Furnace Creek, drive north on Hwy 190 for 17 miles, bear right on Scotty's Castle Road then drive 33 miles to the left turnoff for Ubehebe Crater, which is 5 miles farther
**Tel.**: (760) 786-3200
**Website**: www.nps.gov/deva

**Best season:**
November to April

! Dangerously hot in summer months

**↗ The Mojave fringe-toed lizard lives in sand dunes and has the remarkable ability to breathe under sand.**

Most park visitors stick to the paved roads and main visitor areas of Death Valley, particularly Furnace Creek and Stovepipe Wells. But if you have more than a couple of days to spend in the park, head to Death Valley's northern reaches. Here lie some of the park's most intriguing features, but they come with the price of a long and bumpy drive. North of Ubehebe Crater, the pavement ends and the dirt roads begin. If you choose to venture into this region, make sure your car tires are sturdy and in excellent shape. Also, plan to have plenty of gasoline, water and snacks for the journey. There are no services available, and cell phone service is spotty to nonexistent.

## Ubehebe Crater

Perhaps as recently as 300 years ago, molten lava came in contact with groundwater, steam pressure built up underground, and the earth exploded in a massive volcanic

↑ **Six hundred feet deep and a half mile across, colorful Ubehebe Crater was formed only about 300 years ago.**

belch. When the dust settled, a half-mile-wide, 600-foot-deep crater remained. This colorful hole in the ground, with its striped layers of sedimentary soil, is easily viewed from the park road, just 5 miles from Grapevine Ranger Station. Hike along the trail that follows Ubehebe Crater's southwest rim to several older craters, including Little Hebe. These craters are much smaller, but similar in appearance — mostly black and ash-colored, with eroded walls revealing colorful bands of orange and rust minerals. From Ubehebe's high rim, you can see far off to the Last Chance Range.

## Eureka Dunes

Eureka Dunes are the tallest sand dunes in California and among the tallest in North America. They rise nearly 700 feet from their base, creating a sandy, miniature mountain range that is home to three rare and endangered desert plants — Eureka dunegrass, shining milk vetch and the

↑↗ **The Eureka Dunes are among the tallest sand dunes in North America, rising nearly 700 feet from their base.**

night-blooming Eureka Dunes evening primrose, which is pollinated by moths that fly only at night. These plants' entire range is limited to this single sand patch.

The dunes lie in the remote Eureka Valley, covering an area only 3 miles long and 1 mile wide. But their height is astonishing, especially when you're climbing them. Hiking to the top is much harder than it looks — you'll take two steps forward, slide one step back, then repeat the process. The silky soft sand crystals constantly move beneath your feet. From the trailhead, simply head for the clearly visible dunes. Because of the continually shifting desert sand, there is no marked trail, so make your own path. Your best bet is to climb to the top of the tallest dune in sight, then trace a ridgeline path from dune to dune.

## The Racetrack

Can rocks move? In Death Valley, they can. At "The Racetrack," see the tracks of rocks that have slid along

↑ **At the Racetrack, it's hard to believe what you're seeing: the furrowed imprints of rocks that have traveled across the frozen playa (dry lake bed). Scientists filmed the sliding rocks for the first time in 2014.**

the slick surface of mudflats, pushed by strong winds. This intriguing sight lies at the end of a 26-mile stretch of gravel road, so be prepared for a bone-rattling drive. But it's worth it when you finally reach the vast, flat, white playa where moving rocks have been leaving tracks for eons, some as long as 1,500 feet. In 2014, scientists unraveled the source of the mystery — a combination of wind and melting ice makes the rocks slide across the playa. Strong winds of 50 miles per hour or more can push boulders as large as basketballs weighing up to 500 pounds. It happens only rarely when storm conditions are just right, but the rocks' tracks reveal the story.

## Ubehebe Peak

If you've driven all the way to the Racetrack, you might want to stretch your legs and get some exercise. You'll get it on this 3-mile uphill hike to the 5,678-foot summit of Ubehebe Peak. The trail is a narrow miners' route that offers continually expanding views of the Racetrack playa. From the saddle below the summit, you gain an inspiring view of both the snowy Sierra Nevada and the arid Last Chance Range, as well as the Racetrack and Saline valleys.

# Alabama Hills

***A breathtaking juxtaposition of glacially carved summits and rugged desert geology***

## Hot Spot Highlights

- Hike to a series of wind-sculpted granite arches.
- Photograph whimsical boulder piles and badlands against the contrasting vista of 14,505-foot Mount Whitney.
- Explore the filming site of numerous Hollywood westerns.

**Addresses**: The Arch Trail trailhead, Movie Flat Road, Lone Pine, CA;
Bureau of Land Management Bishop Field Office (visitor center), 351 Pacu Lane, Suite 100, Bishop, CA
**Tel.**: (760) 872-5000
**Website**: www.blm.gov/visit/alabama-hills

**Best season:**
October to April

**↗ The soaring crest of the Sierra Nevada — including Mount Whitney, the lower 48 states' highest peak — frames the Alabama Hills' rounded rock formations and sagebrush plains.**

A maze of rounded granitic boulders, golden-hued arches and badland gullies made Lone Pine's Alabama Hills an ideal backdrop for Hollywood westerns. Filmmakers from the early 20th century loved the way the smooth, weathered boulder piles struck a contrasting pose against a background of jagged Sierra Nevada peaks. This uniquely sculpted geology set the scene for more than a century's worth of movies and television shows, starting with the 1920 Fatty Arbuckle silent film *The Roundup*.

Movie buffs can stop in Lone Pine at the Beverly and Jim Rogers Museum of Lone Pine Film History to pick up the Movie Road Self-Guided Tour booklet (and check out the costumes, saddles, guns and other Hollywood props). A drive on smooth dirt roads leads to Movie Flat and an assortment of spots where Roy Rogers, John Wayne, Gary Cooper, Humphrey Bogart and Hopalong Cassidy ambushed outlaws from their craggy hideouts.

Nature lovers and photographers will want to wander more freely in this land of geological contrasts, searching out the perfect spot to frame a photo of 14,505-foot Mount Whitney, tallest peak in the contiguous United States. Pay homage to this mountain behemoth on the Arch Loop Trail, where Mount Whitney is framed within the twisted span of Mobius Arch. The arch is one of dozens of natural arches that can be found amid the Alabama Hills. Close to Mobius Arch are Lathe Arch, Heart Arch, and the Eye of Alabama. Walk to them all in less than two miles.

Although the Alabama Hills' rounded formations look much different from their close neighbors, the Sierra Nevada's saw-toothed granite peaks, the two were formed by the same forces — a massive uplift of Earth's crust about 100 million years ago. The formations simply eroded in different ways: the Sierra Nevada was weathered by freezing and thawing, whereas the Alabamas were subjected to eons of wind-blown sand, wearing them down to round and smooth shapes.

Wildflower fans start arriving here in March and April to seek out a few rare finds among the Mojave aster, Fremont gold, bush sunflower and scarlet milk vetch. The Inyo County star tulip and Owens Valley checkerbloom can be found near seeps and springs. In some years, the Alabamas' sagebrush plains showcase the brilliant blue of wild hyacinth, a plant whose bulb was coveted food for the Owens Valley Indians.

Free, dispersed camping is permitted for up to 14 days in the Alabama Hills. There is no water or facilities; pack in what you pack out. Nearby Tuttle Creek Campground has 80 developed campsites for tents, RVs and trailers, and several motels and restaurants are located in nearby Lone Pine.

**↑ Mobius Arch is one of dozens of natural arches found in the Alabama Hills, a colorful expanse of granite and metamorphic rock.**

Santa Clarita
Ventura
Simi Valley
Oxnard
Thousand Oaks
Calabasas
Glendale
Pasadena
Rancho Cucamonga
San Bernardino
Fontana
Ontario
Los Angeles
Inglewood
Riverside
Moreno Valley
Corona
Torrance
Anaheim
Garden Grove
Santa Ana
Long Beach
Huntington Beach
Irvine
Palm Desert
Murrieta
Pacific Ocean
Oceanside
Vista
Carlsbad
Escondido
Del Mar
La Jolla
El Cajon
Pine Valley
San Diego
Chula Vista
Mexico
N
S
E
W

# Southern Coast and Mountains

# Channel Islands National Park

***Five islands off the Southern California coast comprise one of America's least-visited and hardest-to-access national parks***

## Hot Spot Highlights

- Camp and hike on remote islands off the Southern California coast.
- Kayak around hundreds of sea caves on Anacapa and Santa Cruz islands.
- See the rare and endemic island fox and Santa Cruz Island scrub jay.
- Visit the largest pinniped rookery in the world at San Miguel Island.

**Address**: Robert J. Lagomarsino Visitor Center, 1901 Spinnaker Drive, Ventura, CA
**Tel.**: (805) 658-5730
**Website**: www.nps.gov/chis

**Best season:**
Year-round

**↗ The Santa Cruz Island scrub jay, a striking blue and white bird with a harsh, raucous cry, lives on this one island and nowhere else in the world.**

Revered for its endemic plants and plentiful wildlife, the "Galapagos of California" has no lodgings, stores or restaurants. Visiting here requires traveling by boat or small plane, then relying on your hiking boots or kayak to get around. But you won't regret the extra effort. A trip to this chain of islands, five of which are part of Channel Islands National Park, is a chance to see the California coast as it was hundreds of years ago.

Each of the five islands — Anacapa, Santa Cruz, Santa Barbara, Santa Rosa and San Miguel — has its own distinct geography and assets. Ocean vistas and rugged coastlines are common to all, but flora and fauna vary. The Channel Islands' most enchanting mammal is the island fox, which resides here and nowhere else on earth. The gray- and rust-colored creature is a much smaller descendent of the mainland gray fox, about the size of a house cat. Three islands have their own unique subspecies of fox, with unique evolutionary adaptations such as a shorter tail or a longer nose. In 2004, each island fox subspecies was federally listed as endangered, but a captive breeding program saved this species from extinction. More than 1,000 island fox now live on Santa Cruz Island.

A huge variety of birds can be seen on the islands. Most of the world's population of Xantus' murrelets, more than half of the world's population of ashy storm petrels, and the only nesting populations of brown pelicans along the

↑ **In February and March, Anacapa Island's giant coreopsis bloom with brilliance. The rest of the year, the plant is decidedly dull, often shedding its leaves so that it's just a clump of wooden stems.**

U.S. West Coast are found here. The Channel Islands also have an endemic species, the Santa Cruz Island scrub jay.

Spring wildflower shows are a major attraction, with blossoms ranging from showy California poppies to subtler manifestations, like the butter-yellow clusters of soft-leaved paintbrush. The latter, endemic to the island chain, is now found only on Santa Rosa Island. In February and March, flower aficionados covet the giant coreopsis — or "tree sunflower" — which grows up to 6 feet tall on Anacapa and Santa Barbara islands. In exceptional years, Anacapa's bushy yellow coreopsis bloom so prolifically that their glow can be seen from the mainland, 12 miles distant.

Arrange boat transportation to the islands in advance. Island Packers (www.islandpackers.com)

runs trips to all five islands from Ventura or Oxnard. Most trips visit only one island at a time. The closest islands — and the ones best suited for single-day trips — are Anacapa and Santa Cruz. Multiday trips that visit more than one island are available from a Santa Barbara–based company, Truth Aquatics.

### Anacapa Island

Closest to the mainland of all the Channel Islands, tiny Anacapa lies only 12 miles out to sea, requiring a boat ride of less than an hour. The mournful horn of the island's lighthouse — a structure that was built in 1929 to steer ships away from this treacherous shoreline — greets visitors at the largest of Anacapa's three tiny islets. A 2-mile walking trail passes dramatic overlooks at Cathedral Cove and Inspiration Point, where you can gaze at the two smaller Anacapa islets and huge Santa Cruz Island beyond. Beaches on Anacapa are not accessible because the sea cliffs are hundreds of feet high, but on calm days, you can swim at the landing cove. Bring your snorkeling gear so you can look eye-to-eye with orange garibaldis and giant sea kelp. Kayakers can circumnavigate the island and explore more than 30 sea caves.

↑ **A 1929 lighthouse stands sentinel on Anacapa Island, where a jagged coastline harbors more than 30 sea caves.**

## Santa Cruz Island

Only one quarter of Santa Cruz Island is national park land, the rest belongs to the Nature Conservancy. But since Santa Cruz is the largest of all the Channel Islands at 96 miles square and 20 miles long, that one quarter covers a lot of territory. The boat trip to the island is only an hour each way, so day trips are possible, but many visitors prefer to stay overnight at the island's Scorpion Canyon Campground. It's close to Scorpion Bay, a great put-in site for kayakers who want to explore the cave-ridden shoreline.

At the top of most paddlers' lists is a trip to Santa Cruz Island's Painted Cave, one of the largest sea caves in the world. The cave is almost 100 feet wide and extends 1,215 feet into the west end of the island. Once you travel through Painted Cave's yawning mouth, it's pitch black inside, but you'll hear life all around you. Seals and sea lions protest your arrival with a ruckus of barking. Hundreds of seabirds roost in the damp alcoves. (Outfitters lead tours to Painted Cave, and even paddling novices can make the trip.)

If you'd rather hike than paddle, trails start from camp. A short walk leads to Cavern Point, a high promontory where you can scan the sea for passing whales. A 4.6-mile

↑ **San Miguel Island boasts some of the Channel Islands' best beaches, with long expanses of white sand backed by tall dunes.**

round-trip takes you to an overlook above Potato Harbor, a potato-shaped cove edged by rugged cliffs. Sea lions frolic in the kelp forests below. A 7-mile round-trip leads to the cobble- and driftwood-covered beach at Smuggler's Cove. As you wander, keep an eye out for the Santa Cruz Island scrub jay, a bright-blue bird that lives on this island and nowhere else in the world.

## Santa Rosa Island

California's second-largest island, Santa Rosa, provides 84 square miles to explore, and a noticeable lack of crowds. Highlights include long expanses of white sand beaches and a rare stand of Torrey pines. (This island and San Diego are the only two spots where these wind-sculpted conifers grow.) Trails and dirt roads crisscross the island, so it's easy to get around on foot. Rangers lead hikes to Lobo Canyon, which is filled with rare native flora, eroded sandstone formations and embedded fossils. Getting to Santa Rosa Island requires a 3-hour boat ride or a 30-minute flight in a small plane. (Channel Island Aviation departs from Camarillo Airport and lands on this island's small airstrip.) Whether they arrive by sea or air, most visitors stay for a few days at Water Canyon Campground, located near a beautiful 3-mile-long beach.

## San Miguel Island

Just 8 miles long and 4 miles wide, San Miguel Island is part-time home to more than 100,000 seals and sea lions who breed, rest and molt at Point Bennett's beaches. This is considered the largest rookery in the world, with up to five different species present most of the year. Seeing this blubbery spectacle is well worth the 15-mile round-trip hike from the island's harbor. A shorter trail leads to the island's fascinating caliche forest, where the calcium-carbonate sand castings of dead plant roots and trunks stand like frozen statues. High winds and fog are common on the island, but on warm, sunny days, it's possible to swim and snorkel in the tourmaline-colored water at Cuyler Harbor. Getting to San Miguel requires a 4-hour boat ride, so most visitors camp for at least a night or two. Only 30 campers are allowed on San Miguel Island at one time, and only rarely do that many people show up at once.

**↑ Anacapa is a major breeding site for California brown pelicans, so juvenile birds are commonly seen on all the islands.**

**↖ One of California's biggest wildlife shows takes place at Point Bennett on San Miguel Island, where more than 100,000 seals and sea lions breed, rest and molt.**

**↖↖ Endemic to the Channel Islands, the island kit fox is a much smaller relative of the mainland gray fox.**

# Santa Monica Mountains National Recreation Area

***A mosaic of state, local and federal preserves protects this rugged open space, the nation's largest urban national park***

### Hot Spot Highlights

- Hike sandstone peaks and shady canyons in the nation's largest urban national park.
- Take in views of the Pacific coast, the Channel Islands and downtown LA from high overlooks.
- See spring wildflowers carpet the slopes and coyotes gallop across the grassy swales.

**Address**: Santa Monica Mountains National Recreation Area, 26876 Mulholland Hwy, Calabasas, CA
**Tel.**: (805) 370-2301
**Website**: www.nps.gov/samo

**Best season:**
Year-round

**↗ Coyotes are well adapted to urban living, but in the Santa Monica Mountains, they have fence-free room to roam.**

Think there's no country left in Los Angeles? Think again. The Santa Monica Mountains stretch for 50 miles across the northwestern boundary of the Los Angeles Basin. Within the range lie more than 150,000 largely undeveloped acres of grassy swales, rock-studded hillsides, tree-shaded glens and windswept beaches. The land is cooperatively managed under the umbrella of Santa Monica Mountains National Recreation Area.

One of the few mountain ranges in the United States that runs east to west, rather than north to south, the Santa Monicas have an impressive résumé of natural wonders. Considered to be a "botanical island" amid LA's urban corridor, the slopes that run straight down to the Pacific are covered in chaparral, coastal sage and oak and sycamore forests. Many threatened and endangered plants and animals make their homes here, including the California red-legged frog. In a single day, you might see a

bobcat stalk its prey, a coyote lope across the grasslands, or a golden eagle fly overhead.

With dozens of possible access points, the hardest part of visiting the Santa Monica Mountains is deciding where to go. The range is bisected by scenic roads, so it's possible to witness some of its charms from behind your windshield. For a driving tour, cruise along Mulholland Drive and Mulholland Highway from Hollywood west to Malibu, or drive Kanan Dume Road north from Malibu to Agoura Hills.

To see the beauty at a slower pace, get out and take a hike. More than 500 miles of trails lace the mountains, including the 67-mile Backbone Trail, an unbroken footpath that makes it possible to backpack for a week in LA's wild outback. Shorter treks are possible too: from the Circle X Ranch trailhead, head to the summit of 3,111-foot Sandstone Peak, the highest point in the recreation area. The vista takes in a wide expanse of island-dotted Pacific and a sweep of downtown's jagged skyline. Go there

**↑ A hike through Cheeseboro Canyon's golden meadows will make you forget you're in the midst of LA's urban corridor.**

**↓ The California red-legged frog is the largest native frog in the western United States, and it is found almost exclusively in California.**

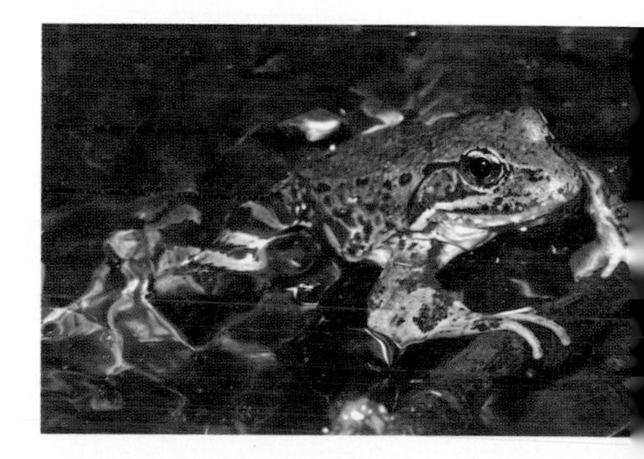

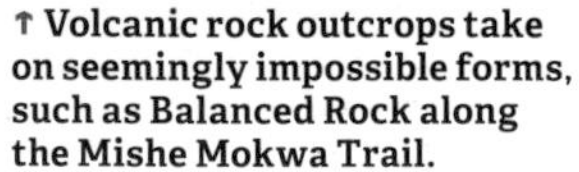

↑ **Volcanic rock outcrops take on seemingly impossible forms, such as Balanced Rock along the Mishe Mokwa Trail.**

↗ **High points in the Santa Monica Mountains deliver vistas of the wild, blue Pacific and the skyscrapers of downtown Los Angeles.**

directly on a 1.5-mile jaunt up the Backbone Trail, or take a more interesting 6-mile loop up the Mishe Mokwa Trail to aptly named Split Rock, then return on Backbone.

In Solstice Canyon, take an easy walk along an oak- and sycamore-shaded creek to the Roberts Ranch stone ruins, once an architecturally grand home that hosted a private zoo where giraffes, camels and exotic birds roamed. At King Gillette Ranch in Calabasas, visit the national park visitor center for maps and information, then take a short, steep tromp to Inspiration Point for views of Malibu Creek State Park's volcanic rock formations.

Thanks to Los Angeles' mild weather, these mountains are easily accessible year-round. But visit in spring and you'll see these parklands at their most colorful. Malibu's Point Mugu State Park is a mecca for wildflower lovers. Hike the

↑ **The Santa Monica Mountains offer more than 500 miles of trails to explore, including the 67-mile Backbone Trail, which crosses the range from east to west.**

Chumash Trail uphill from Pacific Coast Highway — in the lower stretches, you'll see poppies, lupine and mariposa lilies, while up higher you'll find the more exotic chocolate lily and blue globe gilia. The woodlands and grasslands of Topanga State Park light up with dove lupine, blue-eyed grass, blue dicks, fiesta flower and buttercups. Look for the Santa Catalina mariposa lily, a purple-tinted variation of the more common white variety.

Or visit Charmlee Wilderness Park for its spring flower show, plus sweeping views of the Pacific coast, including six of the Channel Islands.

The Santa Monicas are in the middle of a major urban area, so you have a wide range of choices for lodging, dining and supplies. Several state parks nearby offer camping: Leo Carrillo State Park, Point Mugu State Park and Malibu Creek State Park.

# Sand to Snow National Monument

***A newly designated federal parkland spans from the low-elevation desert to 11,503-foot Mount San Gorgonio***

## Hot Spot Highlights

- Look for bighorn sheep, tortoises and other desert wildlife.
- Birdwatch in a willow- and cottonwood-lined wetland.
- Hike or backpack to the top of Southern California's highest peak.

**Addresses**: The Wildlands Conservancy, 39611 Oak Glen Road, Oak Glen, CA;
Mill Creek Visitor Center, 34701 Mill Creek Road, Mentone, CA
**Tel.**: (909) 797-8507 or (909) 382-2882
**Websites**: www.fs.fed.us/visit/sand-to-snow-national-monument, www.blm.gov/visit/sand-to-snow-national-monument, www.wildlandsconservancy.org, www.bigmorongo.org

**Best season:**
November to April for desert regions,
May to October for San Gorgonio

With a swipe of the presidential pen, a huge swath of California desert was granted national monument status in 2016, protecting 1.8 million acres of land for future generations. President Barack Obama's three new national monuments were named after the scenery they preserve: Sand to Snow, Mojave Trails and Castle Mountains. They link with other protected areas — Santa Rosa and San Jacinto National Monument to the south, Joshua Tree National Park to the east, Mojave National Preserve to the north and Death Valley National Park to the northwest — to create a wildlife corridor for desert-dwelling creatures like California's state reptile, the desert tortoise, as well as bighorn sheep and burrowing owls.

The largest of the three new

monuments, Sand to Snow includes a mosaic of parklands spread out over nearly 100 miles of desert and mountains. It's the most biologically diverse of any of America's national monuments, boasting more than 800 types of plants, more than 240 bird species and 12 threatened and endangered species. And these are not just desert flora and fauna. Sand to Snow contains a majority of Southern California's black bear habitat and the state's southernmost stand of quaking aspen trees.

See the "sandy" region of Sand to Snow at Whitewater Canyon Preserve, an easy stop off Interstate 10 west of Palm Springs. Hike along the Whitewater River's wash (which roars with snowmelt in spring, but may be dry in summer) to Red Dome, a ruddy-colored hill created by volcanic action. For a heart-pumping ascent,

**↑ At 11,503 feet, Mount San Gorgonio is Southern California's tallest peak and a mecca for backpackers and hikers.**

**↖ California's state reptile, the desert tortoise, only rarely shows its face outside its underground burrow.**

follow the 3.8-mile Canyon Loop Trail that climbs nearly 1,000 feet for big views of the surrounding peaks. The loop follows a section of the Pacific Crest Trail on its epic journey from Mexico to Canada. Spring wildflowers explode with color along this trail in March and April, especially after a rainy winter.

Another access point for Sand to Snow is at Morongo Valley's Big Morongo Canyon Preserve, an oasis for bird lovers. Nearly 250 avian species have been spotted at this junglelike wetland surrounding Big Morongo Creek. Song sparrows, house finches and hummingbirds whiz past as you follow the wooden boardwalks of the Mesquite Trail through a marshy maze of willows and cottonwoods. Birdwatchers come from around the world to this Pacific Flyway stop and are sometimes rewarded with rare sightings, like the vermilion flycatcher or endangered least Bell's vireo.

The snowy face of Sand to Snow is visible in winter on 11,503-foot Mount San Gorgonio, Southern California's highest peak and a magnet for peak-baggers. The bald summit, affectionately called Old Grayback, crowns the San Gorgonio Wilderness, an alpine wonderland of firs, pines, waterfalls, meadows and small lakes. To visit,

**↑ In spring, bright yellow brittlebush transforms Whitewater Canyon's subdued face with its show-stopping color.**

**← The vermilion flycatcher is a coveted prize on any birder's life list — and you might just spot one at Morongo Canyon.**

drive to the town of Forest Falls in the San Bernardino Mountains, then take a hike on the Vivian Creek Trail. You'll need snowshoes in winter and hiking boots in summer. A grueling 8.5-mile trek leads to mighty San Gorgonio's summit, a trip best split into two days, thanks to a butt-kicking 5,000-foot elevation gain. Several camps offer backpackers a place to rest: Vivian Creek Camp at 1.2 miles, Halfway Camp at 2.5 miles and High Creek Camp at 4.8 miles. On the clearest days, Old Grayback's summit offers a mind-boggling view of Southern California, the vista extending as far as Mount Whitney, 190 miles away.

Day-hikers can wander for a couple of miles up Mill Creek Canyon, enjoying the free-flowing stream and alpine scenery. Along the way is Big Falls — Southern California's tallest waterfall at 500 feet high — which drops into Falls Creek. From this trail, you can see only its top tier, a splashy drop of about 150 feet that cascades down into Mill Creek Canyon.

**↑ During peak snowmelt, Big Falls roars as it cascades hundreds of feet into Mill Creek Canyon.**

**↖ The Whitewater River's wide and ebullient springtime flow comes as a surprise to first-time visitors.**

# Santa Rosa Plateau Ecological Reserve

***A rare ecosystem of vernal pools that come to life in the rainy season***

## Hot Spot Highlights

- See rare plants and animals thrive in vernal pools.
- Hike among native bunchgrass and rare Engelmann oaks.
- Watch for deer, coyote and bobcats.

**Address**: Santa Rosa Plateau Ecological Reserve, 39400 Clinton Keith Road, Murrieta, CA
**Tel.**: (951) 677-6951
**Website**: www.rivcoparks.org

**Day use only**

**Best season:**
October to April (February and March for vernal pools)

**↗ Blue dicks, or wild hyacinth, sport a cluster of purple blossoms at the end of a long, single stem.**

Ten miles north of the winery-rich region of Temecula lie some of Southern California's last remaining vernal pools, rare wetland systems unique to the Golden State. These ephemeral pools are created where an impression in hard ground allows rainwater to pool for several weeks during the winter. The ponds do not last — water arrives during the rainy season, then dries up soon thereafter, and the pools remain dry until the following winter. Amazingly, specially adapted plants and animals have evolved to survive these yearly extremes of flood and drought; they are able to thrive in a totally dry, then suddenly aquatic environment. A single vernal pool typically supports 15 to 20 species that can live only in this type of habitat.

The 9,000-acre Santa Rosa Plateau Ecological Reserve was established to preserve its vernal pools plus several other important ecological features,

including the rare Engelmann oak. The reserve also contains some of California's finest remaining bunchgrass prairie.

In February or March, your first sojourn should be the 1-mile walk on the Vernal Pool Trail (start from the trailhead 2 miles west of the visitor center on Clinton Keith Road). A trail through the grasslands leads to a boardwalk travers-ing a wide, shallow, basalt-lined pool, the reserve's largest. Get down on your hands and knees to look closely at this fragile ecosystem, and you may be able to spot fairy shrimp — tiny and amazing crustaceans that hatch from cysts, not eggs — which have been living in a state of suspended animation since

the previous winter. You'll also hear a cacophony of mating frogs. Two-striped garter snakes arrive en masse to feast on frog tadpoles, and birds use the vernal pools as a rest and feeding stop. Wildflowers ringing the pools creep toward the center as the water evaporates in April or May. Most flowers don't begin to bloom until the water is almost gone.

The reserve's first-rate visitor center offers ranger-led interpretive hikes to the vernal pools and the 1846 Moreno and Machado adobes, which served as cowboy bunkhouses. The buildings evoke the history of California's pre-state era, when Spanish Land Grant rancheros ruled the land.

During the dry season, hike from the visitor center through a grove of Engelmann oaks to the top of Monument Hill (elevation 2,046 feet), the reserve's highest point. The vista extends near and far. The park's chaparral- and cactus-covered hills and rolling grasslands line the foreground while the background is dotted with classic Southern California landmarks: Mounts San Gorgonio, San Jacinto and Palomar; Cuyamaca Peak and Mount Woodson in San Diego; the high summits of the San Gabriel Mountains; and even the distant Pacific Ocean.

The nearby towns of Murrieta and Temecula offer lodgings, restaurants and groceries.

**↑ The Engelmann oak is semi-deciduous, losing its leaves only during drought periods.**

**↖ This ephemeral vernal pool may last for only a month or so, but it supports more than a dozen species that can live only in this part-time dry, part-time wet environment.**

# Laguna Mountain Recreation Area

***San Diego's alpine mountains offer dense forests and winter snow next to contrasting desert vistas***

## Hot Spot Highlights

- Hike a section of the epic Pacific Crest Trail.
- Climb to the summit of Garnet Peak.
- Witness spectacular sunsets and sunrises.
- Play in the snow in sunny San Diego County.

**Address**: Laguna Mountain Visitor Center, Los Huecos Road, Mt Laguna, CA
**Tel.**: (619) 473-8547 or (619) 445-6235
**Website**: www.fs.usda.gov/cleveland/

**Best season:**
Year-round

**↗ Wedged into cracks and crevices wherever its roots can find a bit of soil, this Laguna Mountains sedum produces white, daisy-like flowers.**

Most people associate San Diego County with sunshine and palm-tree-lined beaches, but in its eastern reaches, the county boasts a small mountain range with elevations as high as Lake Tahoe's alpine shores (6,200 feet). The pine-studded Laguna Mountains see a few inches of snowfall almost every winter. Year-round, the range's high peaks and ridges deliver astonishing vistas, especially of the far-below Anza-Borrego Desert. Plan a sunrise hike here, or spend the night in a tent and get up early, and you'll see a sublime sky turning gold and pink in the dawn light.

The Laguna Mountain Recreation Area is bisected by the Sunrise Highway, Route S-1, offering easy access to numerous hiking trails, including a section of the 2,650-mile Pacific Crest Trail, which runs from Mexico to Canada. For a quick taste of what this area has to offer, drive to the

Pioneer Mail Picnic Area, the site of a historic stagecoach route, and walk to Kwaaymii Point, one of the best spots in the Lagunas for knock-your-socks-off views of the Anza-Borrego Desert. The wide, half-mile stretch of trail chiseled into the cliff was once the roadbed of the Sunrise Highway. Or take a longer hike to Garnet Peak.

A National Forest Adventure Pass is required for your vehicle ($5 per day). Purchase one at the Cleveland National Forest visitor center or Laguna Mountain Lodge. The lodge offers rooms and cabins for

↑ An easy hike leads to the summit of Garnet Peak, where the vast desert spreads out thousands of feet below.

overnight stays. Two Forest Service-run campgrounds offer tent and RV sites: Laguna and Burnt Rancheria.

## Garnet Peak

A 4-mile hike on the famous Pacific Crest Trail leads to the summit of Garnet Peak and one of San Diego County's best desert viewpoints. Start at the Penny Pines trailhead and follow the PCT north (left). The trail hugs the Laguna Mountains' eastern rim, offering nearly nonstop views of Storm Canyon and the Anza-Borrego Desert. At a junction at 1.5 miles, turn right and head uphill to the top of the 5,900-foot peak. Garnet Peak's escarpment falls away dramatically to the east and south, offering up a full 360-degree view that includes not only the vast desert thousands of feet below, but also Mount San Jacinto and Mount San Gorgonio, the Cuyamaca Mountains, the Salton Sea, the "white golf ball" of Palomar Observatory and more. Look closely at the summit's tan-colored rocks and you may see the tiny reddish-colored crystals that give this mountain its name.

# Torrey Pines State Natural Reserve

***The world's rarest pine tree flourishes in this coastal reserve***

## Hot Spot Highlights

- See one of the world's rarest pine species.
- Wander the Pacific-view blufftops, surrounded by wildflowers.
- Hike through coastal badlands to the beach.

**Address**: Torrey Pines State Natural Reserve, 12600 N. Torrey Pines Road, La Jolla, CA
**Tel.**: (858) 755-2063
**Websites**: www.torreypines.org, www.parks.ca.gov/?page_id=657

**Day use only**

**Best season:**
Year-round

**↗ Steep, eroded badlands descend to the cerulean ocean at Torrey Pines State Natural Reserve.**

On rugged bluffs bisected by steep, eroded ravines grows the world's rarest pine tree, the Torrey pine. This twisted, gnarled conifer exists only here at San Diego's Torrey Pines State Reserve and on Santa Rosa Island, off the coast of Santa Barbara. Visit this reserve to pay homage to the trees — only about 10,000 remain in the world — and also to enjoy gentle hiking paths and breathtaking Pacific vistas.

Torrey Pines' botanical bragging rights extend to more than just its trees. More than 350 plant species have been identified within the relatively small (1,750 acres) reserve. Stop in at the visitor center and museum to learn about the native succulents, chaparral plants and wildflowers that grace this oceanfront bluff. Or wander through the Whitaker Native Plant Garden, where many species are labeled, including the endangered Shaw's agave, a needle-sharp agave that produces nectar for bees. The garden lies at the top of Parry Grove Trail's 118 stone steps, which travel downhill (and then back up) to coastal viewpoints.

Nearby, the Guy Fleming Trail provides more sweeping vistas of the Pacific Ocean and Los Peñasquitos Marsh, but on a much easier grade. In spring, a brilliant display of coastal wildflowers emblazon the blufftops. Hike the loop's right side first to access the North Overlook, then circle around to the South Overlook. On the clearest days, you can pick out San Clemente and Catalina Islands, some 70 miles away in the wind-ruffled Pacific. Fifteen-foot-high Torrey pines, their branches contorted by salty air and stiff ocean breezes, frame the scene.

For a longer walk, follow Razor Point Trail for views of the reserve's dramatically eroded coastal badlands. Stop at Red Butte, a massive sandstone outcrop that

offers a commanding view of the Pacific. Head south from Razor Point to connect to Beach Trail, then squeeze through a narrow sandstone notch to access the beach. After a stroll along the sand, return the way you came, or for a longer hike, head back uphill on Broken Hill Trail.

The small parking lot at Torrey Pines fills up early, especially on weekends, so arrive early in the day to get a spot or plan on walking a mile up the hill from the beach parking lots. Lodgings, restaurants and groceries are in plentiful supply in Del Mar and La Jolla.

**↑ One of the world's rarest pines, the graceful Torrey pine lives in only two places in the world, Torrey Pines State Natural Reserve and Santa Rosa Island.**

**← Shaw's agave is a rare native agave species that is found in only a few places along the San Diego coast, usually on the edge of eroding bluffs.**

# Cabrillo National Monument

***A coastal Mediterranean climate supports some of Southern California's best tide pools***

## Hot Spot Highlights

- Explore tide pools teeming with life.
- Hike through coastal Mediterranean habitat.
- Watch for passing gray whales on their annual migration.

**Address**: Cabrillo National Monument, 1800 Cabrillo Memorial Drive, San Diego, CA
**Tel.**: (619) 557-5450
**Website**: www.nps.gov/cabr

**Day use only**

**Best season:**
January and February for whale watching

**↗ Ochre sea stars are making a comeback on the Pacific coast after a massive virus in 2013 nearly wiped them out. In tide pools, look for them clinging to rocks in the splash zone.**

**↗↗ Every whale watcher hopes for the chance to see a gray whale spy-hop, or shoot out of the water vertically by kicking with its tail. Whales do this in order to see their surroundings.**

Cabrillo National Monument commemorates the courage and vision of Juan Rodriguez Cabrillo, the Spanish explorer who was the first European to set foot on America's west coast. His statue towers over a magnificent view of San Diego Bay and a significant chunk of San Diego's coveted waterfront real estate. No mega-mansions or condominiums clutter this seaside blufftop — just a glass-domed lighthouse, a walking trail through splendid coastal Mediterranean habitat and a rocky intertidal zone with tide pools bursting with sea creatures.

To fully enjoy Cabrillo's spectacular tide pool area, check your tide table before you visit and aim to arrive during the three-hour window that brackets the lowest tide of the day. Minus tides (tides below zero feet) provide the best viewing. Walk the beach to look for mussels, crabs, sea hares, barnacles, sea stars, bat stars, anemones, snails and limpets. If you're lucky, you might see an octopus or a sea urchin. For a brief lesson on intertidal creatures, drive up the hill to the visitor center and watch the film in the auditorium.

Also atop the hill is a paved trail that leads to the Old Point Loma Lighthouse. Look inside to see its 19th-century period furniture and imagine what daily life was like for the hardworking light keeper and his family. The building's exterior view is a major draw — this high plateau is a great spot to watch for gray whale spouts as they pass by in January and February, returning from their breeding grounds in Baja California, Mexico. More than 25,000 gray whales swim past this point each year.

Take a walk on the Bayside Trail to enjoy blue-water views and classic coastal sagebrush habitat. This coastal Mediterranean ecosystem is one

of the eight most sensitive in the world. The trail curves downhill around Point Loma, and with every step, the whole of San Diego Bay and the Pacific Ocean are yours to survey. Huge navy ships head out to sea, flocks of gulls follow fishing boats into the harbor and sailboats seem to dance across the bay's surface. Interpretive signs identify sage scrub, marine chaparral and succulents and describe local and migrating birds. Hummingbirds buzz through the flora — Indian paintbrush, aromatic sages, prickly pear, agaves and buckwheat.

The parking lot at the tide pool area fills quickly; arrive early to get a spot, or walk a mile downhill from the visitor center parking lot. The city of San Diego offers myriad options for dining and lodging, including campgrounds.

**↑ Imagine the life of a 19th-century lighthouse keeper as you stroll through the rooms of the Old Point Loma Lighthouse.**

**↑↑ Layered sandstone edges the tide pool area at Cabrillo National Monument.**

Nevada
N
S
E
W
Kern R.
Bakersfield
Cantil
Kelso
Barstow
Lancaster
Palmdale
Amboy
Santa Clarita
Simi Valley
Thousand Oaks
Glendale
Pasadena
San Bernardino
Fontana
Twentynine Palms
Los Angeles
Oak Glen
Inglewood
Riverside
Moreno Valley
Corona
Anaheim
Torrance
Thousand Palms
Palm Springs
Cathedral City
Long Beach
Santa Ana
Indio
Huntington Beach
Irvine
Costa Mesa
Mecca
Murrieta
Temecula
Pacific Ocean
Borrego Springs
Oceanside
Vista
Carlsbad
Escondido
Julian
1
2
3
4
5
6
7
8
9
10
11
12

# Southern Deserts

# Red Rock Canyon State Park

***A landscape of colorful sandstone formations sculpted by geological forces***

### Hot Spot Highlights

- See wrinkled and folded cliffs in dramatic colors.
- Look for petroglyphs and fossils.
- Attend a star party with amateur astronomers.

**Address**: Red Rock Canyon State Park, 37749 Abbott Drive, Cantil, CA
**Tel.**: (661) 946-6092
**Websites**: www.parks.ca.gov/?page_id=631, www.redrockrrcia.org

**Best season:**
October to April

Dangerously hot in summer months

**In Red Cliffs' twisted and tortured landscape, iron oxide tints the badlands rusty red.**

Once the home of the Kawaiisu Indians, who left petroglyphs in the vividly colored cliffs, and later a gold-mining site, stagecoach stop, railroad route, and backdrop for Hollywood westerns, Red Rock Canyon State Park protects a multihued collection of wrinkled sandstone cliffs and dramatically shaped buttes and outcrops. At the edge of the El Paso Range, a series of eroded badlands rise up from the sandy soil, their creases and folds sculpted by eons of wind and water erosion. Photographers gather at sunrise and sunset, trying to capture the whites, pinks, reds and browns at their most saturated. Paleontologists flock here too. In the cliffs' sediments are the remains of prehistoric animals — three-toed horses, saber-toothed cats and alligator lizards. Ninety species of fossilized plants and animals have been documented in Red Rock Canyon.

Take a walk among the furrowed formations of Hagen Canyon and Red Cliffs. At Red Cliffs, a path leads between the columns of 300-foot-high desert monoliths, their red

tint caused by iron oxide (rust). It's hard to imagine, but this entire region was under water 10 million years ago. Sediment flowed downhill from the surrounding mountains and was deposited in layers at the bottom of an ancient lake, creating these stratified formations. After a wet winter, spring wildflowers erupt in a riot of color. Flower fans come here in search of the Red Rock poppy, a rare and possibly endangered species.

Across the highway at Hagen Canyon, a 1.2-mile nature trail leads past more outrageously colored and sculpted badlands, plus a

↑ **Humans are dwarfed by the soaring cliffs near Ricardo Campground, the rock faces sculpted by wind and water erosion.**

smattering of Joshua trees. Each colorful layer or strata tells a geologic story: red for sandstone that was deposited in stream and river channels, white for sandstone that was subjected to ash from volcanic eruptions, and gray for sandstone that was deposited in huge floodplains. Some of the fluted cliffs look like colorful candles melting in the sun. Others have small caves or "windows," inviting children (and adults) to climb and explore.

The park's beauty doesn't end at sunset. Located 125 miles from the night-sky-polluting lights of Los Angeles, Red Rock Canyon offers astronomy buffs blissfully dark nights. The park's Ricardo Campground is often dotted with telescopes. The China Lake Astronomical Society holds star parties. On most Saturday nights, docents give talks on astronomy, petroglyphs, desert tortoises, Joshua trees, mining history and more.

Red Rock Canyon is a long way from the nearest large town, so make sure your car is stocked with gas, water and snacks. The town of California City is the best bet for groceries, meals and lodging. Campsites are available at the park's 50-site Ricardo Campground.

# Antelope Valley California Poppy Reserve

***Hills carpeted by swaths of California poppies and other wildflowers***

## Hot Spot Highlights

- See an astounding display of golden California poppies.
- Hike eight miles of undulating grassland trails.

**Address**: Antelope Valley California Poppy Reserve, 15101 W. Lancaster Road, Lancaster, CA
**Tel.**: (661) 724-1180 or (661) 724-1206
**Website**: www.parks.ca.gov/?page_id=627

**Day use only**

**Best season:**
Mid-March to early May

**↗ The poppies steal the show at Antelope Valley, but they're joined by other wildflowers, including goldfields, cream cups and lupine.**

Every spring, an eye-popping show takes place in the far northeast corner of Los Angeles County: the hills west of Lancaster burst into a Technicolor display of California poppies, their silky orange petals embracing the warm spring air. If flowers were gold, the Antelope Valley California Poppy Reserve would be an embarrassment of riches.

But to witness the flower power of *Eschscholzia californica*, you must strategize. Timing is everything with these flowers, and the peak bloom period changes from year to year. Usually the show starts in early April, but it can take place any time between mid-March and early May.

For status updates, check the state reserve's website, which is updated weekly. And when it's go-time, don't procrastinate. Even when the poppies are blooming with gusto, they can disappear in a few days if there's a sudden heat wave.

California's beloved state flower is micromanaged by a committee — sun, clouds, heat and wind. If it's too cold or windy, the poppies close up. Mid-morning is usually the best time to arrive at the preserve because the air warms

↑ **Antelope Valley explodes into bloom every spring, but when a "superbloom" occurs, the reserve shows off an embarrassment of flowery riches.**

up enough for the poppies to open, but the afternoon winds haven't kicked in yet.

Seven miles of trails lace the reserve. Most visitors stick to the 2.5-mile South and North Loop trail with a quick side trip to the Tehachapi Vista Point, but the best displays may or may not be there. Stop in at the visitor center to get the latest updates on where the most flowers are blooming. Docents offer free guided walks on most days.

A California study in the 1960s proved that the western end of Antelope Valley, situated at 2,800 feet in elevation, possesses the state's most consistent poppy-bearing land, thanks to factors ranging from soil type to annual rainfall. But other wildflowers thrive in this rich earth too. Look for purple lupine and white cream cups dispersed among the fields of gold.

Help to ensure the blooms come back next year by obeying the reserve's rules: stay on the trails at all times. If the poppies get trampled before they can make seeds, it cuts down on the following year's blooms. The nearby town of Lancaster has several options for lodging and dining.

# Mojave National Preserve

***A surprisingly lush desert landscape is home to massive sand dunes, volcanic cliffs and dense Joshua tree forests***

## Hot Spot Highlights

- Climb the third-highest dune system in the United States.
- See one of the world's densest Joshua tree forests.
- Hike through the hole-ridden walls of Banshee Canyon.
- Ascend to the top of a 5,775-foot peak.
- Look for the elusive desert tortoise.

**Address**: Kelso Depot Visitor Center, 90942 Kelso Cima Road, Kelso, CA
**Tel.**: (760) 252-6100
**Websites**: www.nps.gov/moja, www.mojavepreserve.org

**Best season:**
October to April

To drivers speeding by on Interstates 15 or 40, Mojave National Preserve might look bland and inhospitable. But a closer look at this national park unit sandwiched between two desert highways uncovers a wealth of riches: water-sculpted canyons, lava flows, cinder cones, dry lakes, a massive dune field and several small mountain ranges. Located at the junction of the Mojave, Great Basin and Sonoran deserts, Mojave National Preserve encompasses geological wonders including gleaming sand dunes, a massive symmetrical dome covered with Joshua trees and volcanic cliffs.

Your first stop should be the Mojave's excellent visitor center, housed in the renovated Kelso Depot, a Spanish-style railroad stop built in 1923. Purchase books and maps and get current road and trail information from the rangers and volunteers stationed there. Then set out to see some of the preserve's most interesting highlights.

California's state reptile, the never-in-a-hurry desert tortoise, is fairly abundant in Mojave National Preserve. This long-lived reptile reaches adulthood between the ages of 14 and 20, and if it can avoid misfortune, it may live to be 80 years old — much like humans. The tortoise is on the threatened species list — not quite endangered but close — and one of its biggest predators is the automobile. Tortoises are most commonly seen in spring, when they emerge from their underground burrows to feed on green grasses and flowers and find a mate. They may also come out after rare summer "monsoon" storms. Look for them near creosote bushes. If you happen to see a tortoise in the wild, do not pick it up — handling wild tortoises is illegal and may be fatal to the tortoise. The only exception is if you see one on a roadway; moving it off to the side (preferably to a shady spot) may save its life.

Mojave National Preserve is remote, so even if you're just visiting for the day, make sure your car is stocked with food, water and gasoline. No services are available in the

↑ **California's state reptile, the desert tortoise, has a lifespan similar to a human's of approximately 80 years.**

preserve, and no large towns are nearby. The park has two developed campgrounds, Hole-in-the-Wall and Mid Hills, each with pit toilets and drinking water. Additionally, primitive roadside camping is permitted throughout the park.

## Kelso Dunes

The most popular sunset and sunrise spot is the Kelso Dunes, the second-largest dune system in California and the third-highest in the United States. These dunes cover 45 square miles and soar to 650 feet. In spring, desert wildflowers such as evening primrose and blazing star add a tapestry of color to the rippling pink white sand. Climb up the face of one of the highest dunes — a short trip but more tiring than you'd expect, thanks to the ever-shifting sand — and you're rewarded with big views of the Granite and Providence Mountains. As you descend, listen carefully to the sand avalanches created by your feet — you might hear a resonant vibration or booming sound, a phenomenon that occurs at only a few of the world's dune complexes. If you don't hear it, listen to a recording of the sound at the Kelso Depot Visitor Center. (The Kelso Dunes Trailhead is 7 miles south of the visitor

center on Kelbaker Road; turn west and drive 2.8 miles on a well-graded dirt road to the trailhead.) Many visitors choose to camp near the Kelso Dunes so they can stay out late or get up early to photograph the dunes at sunset or sunrise.

## Hole-in-the-Wall Hike

The "rings climb" at Hole-in-the-Wall is a must-do hike through the multilayered cliffs and pockmarked boulders of Banshee Canyon, which were formed by volcanic eruptions about 18 million years ago. Gases trapped in the volcanic ash created the eerie-looking holes in the rock.

The canyon was named by early settlers who were awed by the howling desert wind, which reminded them of the shrieking banshee faeries of Celtic lore. On this easy 1.5-mile loop, hikers climb or descend through the twisted passages of Banshee Canyon aided by metal rings hammered into the rock, providing footholds and handholds in the steep sections.

You can walk the loop in either direction; one leg passes through the twisting, colorful canyon and the other travels through a scenic wash lined with tall Mojave yuccas and a cactus garden of barrels, buckhorn cholla and prickly pear. Two longer sojourns are also possible from this canyon: the 6-mile Barber Peak Loop circles the rhyolite cliffs of Barber Peak, and an 8-mile one-way trek leads to Mid Hills

**↑ Gases trapped in volcanic ash from an ancient eruption created the holes in Banshee Canyon's rocks.**

**↖ On the Hole-in-the-Wall hike, metal rings hammered into the rock make it easy to climb up, over and through a series of rocky passages and alcoves.**

**← Kelso Dunes, renowned for their "singing sands," are the third highest dune system in the United States.**

↑ **A lush garden of desert flora dots the slopes of Teutonia Peak, from pancake prickly pear cactus to towering Joshua trees.**

Campground. You'll need to arrange a car shuttle for pickup at the end. The trailhead is located at the picnic area near Hole-in-the-Wall Campground.

## Teutonia Peak

For fans of desert woodland flora, especially the comically angular Joshua tree, it's hard to beat the 3-mile round-trip hike to the top of Teutonia Peak. This high-desert elevation (5,000 feet and up) sees more rainfall than low-desert areas — even occasional snowfall. Precipitation combined with rich, sandy soil have created a nourishing garden plot for the Dr. Seuss–style trees, a member of the fibrous yucca family with spine-tipped leaves. The Joshuas grow larger and more densely

here than in their namesake parkland to the south, Joshua Tree National Park. The first mile of trail passes through one of the densest Joshua tree forests in the world. The trail then connects with a dirt road leading to a few old mine shafts from a silver mine that was first worked in 1896, then again in 1906, then abandoned completely, like so many others in the desert. Beyond the mine, the trail climbs more aggressively to the 5,775-foot summit of Teutonia Peak, which offers an expansive view of surrounding basins and ranges. This rock-studded summit is the highest point on top of Cima Dome, a huge symmetrical dome that stretches for 10 miles at its widest point.

**↑ Substantial precipitation and nourishing soils encourage Joshua trees to soar to heights of 30 feet and up on the lower slopes of Teutonia Peak.**

# Amboy Crater National Natural Landmark

***A broad cinder cone reigns over one of the youngest volcanic fields in the United States***

## Hot Spot Highlights

- Hike to a 6,000-year-old volcanic cinder cone.
- See spring wildflowers carpet the black, hardened lava field.
- Admire desert vistas from the crater rim.

**Address**: Crater Road, Amboy, CA; from Needles, take Interstate 40 west approximately 65 miles to Kelbaker Road, drive south on Kelbaker Road for 10 miles to National Trails Hwy (Route 66), turn left onto National Trails Hwy and drive 8 miles to Crater Road, then turn left
**Tel.**: (760) 326-7000
**Website**: https://www.blm.gov/visit/amboy-crater

**Best season:**
October to April

Just south of Mojave National Preserve sits 1,500-foot-wide Amboy Crater, a volcanic ash and cinder cone that dominates its surrounding 26-mile lava flow. This strange-looking volcanic feature is an example of geology creating geometry — the nearly symmetrical volcanic cinder cone rises 246 feet from the flatlands around it. This is one of the youngest volcanic fields in the United States, created by at least four distinct periods of volcanic eruptions, the most recent occurring about 6,000 years ago.

The hike to the crater is only 1.1 miles one-way but can be hot even in the winter months due to a complete absence of shade. Wear a hat and bring plenty of water, even if the air temperature is cool. A single trail meanders around to the crater's west side, then ascends to its rim via a breach where lava once spewed out. The flow created lava lakes, collapsed lava tubes and sinks, spatter cones and massive flows of mineral-rich basalt. Look closely alongside the trail and you may be able to spot tiny, green-colored olivine crystals. Glimmers of red indicate the presence of ferric iron.

Once on top of the cinder cone, most visitors circumnavigate the 1,508-foot-wide rim, which offers panoramic vistas of the Marble Mountains and the Bristol Mountains, as well as a close-up look at the barren crater floor. Take a moment to study the rocks — some are porous, but others are smooth, a phenomenon caused by the differing amount of steam held in the flowing lava. From the high vantage point of the crater's rim, the desert's enormity comes into perspective: Bristol Dry Lake stretches to the horizon, its calcium chloride still being mined to make "salt" to deice roadways. The tall peaks of Mojave National Preserve lie to the north. Faraway cars moving along the highway look like miniature

toys. Train tracks slice straight lines through the sand.

If possible, time your visit for springtime, when wildflowers push up from the lava field. Look for desert lilies, pink primroses and purple-pink sand verbena in February and March.

Amboy Crater is one of the showpieces of Mojave Trails National Monument, which was designated in 2016. This relatively new national park unit includes the longest undeveloped stretch of historic Route 66, America's "Mother Road," one of the original highways within the U.S. highway system. Much of Route 66 is now abandoned, but you can stop in at the tiny hamlet of Amboy, the self-proclaimed "ghost town that ain't dead yet." It's a rustic time capsule of 1950s Americana.

This region of the Mojave Desert is sparsely populated, so plan accordingly. Gasoline and limited groceries are available in Amboy and Ludlow. Lodging is available in Barstow or Twentynine Palms.

**↑ The desolate interior of the crater is filled with volcanic ash and cinders.**

**↖ An austere landscape created by a lava flow surrounds Amboy Crater, where only a few plants and animals can survive.**

# Joshua Tree National Park Northern Region

***A rock climber's paradise, this park offers geologic wonders and fascinating flora beneath a breathtaking night sky***

## Hot Spot Highlights

- Ascend the park's tallest peak to take in Joshua Tree's grandest view.
- Hike to a palm-studded oasis.
- See the Milky Way stretch across the night sky.
- Climb a rock, or watch the pros do it.
- See the remains of a productive gold mine.

**Addresses**: Joshua Tree Visitor Center, 6554 Park Boulevard, Joshua Tree, CA;
Oasis Visitor Center, 74485 National Park Drive, Twentynine Palms, CA
**Tel.**: (760) 367-5500
**Websites**: www.nps.gov/jotr, www.joshuatree.org

**Best season:**
October to April

**↗ From White Tank Campground, it's a short walk through monzogranite boulder piles to Arch Rock, a photogenic crescent of rock that accentuates the desert sky.**

Joshua Tree contains a whimsical mosaic of boulders and buttresses, rugged mountains, gold mining ruins, and desert plains dotted with the quirky yucca species known as Joshua trees. The park lies at an ecological crossroads, where the high Mojave Desert meets the low Colorado Desert, a part of the much larger Sonoran Desert. The result? A smorgasbord of desert flora comprising 750 varieties of plants. Joshua Tree's beauty shines around the clock, so plan to stay past daylight to witness vibrant sunsets and starry nights.

There is no food service in the park, so make sure your car is well stocked with gas, snacks and especially water. The towns of Yucca Valley, Joshua Tree and Twentynine Palms are located adjacent to Joshua Tree's two major northern entrances (West Entrance at Park Boulevard and North Entrance at Oasis of Mara). For breakfast or lunch, head to

Natural Sisters Café or Crossroads Café. Coffee lovers will find nirvana at Joshua Tree Coffee Company. For dinner, head to Joshua Tree Saloon or get a pizza at Pie for the People. In Twentynine Palms, have a memorable dinner or book a cabin rental at the historic Twentynine Palms Inn.

Of the park's nine campgrounds, four can be reserved at www.recreation.gov up to 6 months in advance of your visit. The most popular, Jumbo Rocks, has 124 sites tucked inside a maze of granite boulders, and an amphitheater for ranger talks held on weekend evenings. Black Rock Campground is popular with families and groups thanks to running water, flush toilets and slightly cooler temperatures. Five more park campgrounds are available on a first-come, first-served basis, but they fill up quickly on weekends.

**↑ The quirky Joshua tree, which is not a tree at all but a yucca, looks like it might have been created by Dr. Seuss.**

**↖ Almost everywhere you look in Joshua Tree, cream-colored boulders, towers, alcoves and spires invite you to explore.**

## Joshua Trees

This spindly, cartoonlike tree, an icon of the high Mojave Desert, grows only in the higher elevations (you won't see them in the park's southern reaches, where the elevations are lower). The park's namesake tree is not a tree at all, but a yucca (*Yucca brevifolia*). Legend maintains that the

tree was named by Mormon settlers in the mid-1800s who said its shape resembled the biblical figure Joshua, reaching his hands to the sky in prayer. Many animals and birds depend on the Joshua tree for food and shelter. The Scott's oriole makes its nest in the branches, woodrats build their nests at the base, lizards search for insects in the fallen branches and the yucca moth lays her eggs inside the creamy white-green flowers. Some of the park's trees are more than 40 feet high — the largest grow in Queen Valley near Black Rock Campground.

## Rock Climbing and Viewing

Massive granite outcrops define the landscape of Joshua Tree almost as much as the park's namesake tree. More than 100 million years ago, seismic activity from the San Andreas Fault forced molten rock upward from Earth's crust. It cooled and hardened below Earth's surface, and over time, flash floods washed away layers of dirt, exposing towers, domes and spires of monzogranite. Large areas of rounded cream-colored boulders with descriptive names like Jumbo Rocks, Wonderland of Rocks and Skull Rock are filled with alcoves and miniature caves that beg to be explored. The boulder fields in Hidden Valley and Lost Horse

Valley — with rocks ranging from only a few feet high to more than 200 feet high — are some of the park's best photography locations. But for simple fun, it's hard to beat the easy walk around the boulders at Skull Rock or Arch Rock.

Given this boulder abundance, Joshua Tree is Southern California's rock climbing mecca. The park's more than 6,000 established climbing routes present diverse challenges ranging from easy beginner slabs to extreme bolted sport routes and vertical cracks. Whether you want to climb or just watch climbers in action, some of the park's best climbing routes are found near Hidden Valley and Ryan campgrounds and at the vast Wonderland of Rocks. The longest technical climbing routes in the park are located at Saddle Rocks, west of Ryan Mountain. Local guide services offer instruction for climbers of all levels.

## Ryan Mountain

Ryan Mountain provides a spectacular view that showcases Queen Valley, Wonderland of Rocks, Lost Horse Valley, Pleasant Valley and the high alpine peaks of Mount San Gorgonio and Mount San Jacinto. To see it, hike 1.5 miles uphill through big boulders

↑ Pancake prickly pear cacti are cloaked in golden spines that glow in the afternoon sun.

↖ The trail to the summit of Ryan Mountain offers spectacular views from Joshua Tree's tallest peak.

← Several guide services offer rock climbing classes on Joshua Tree's spectacular spires, domes and towers.

↑ **The Mojave yucca, a member of the agave family that's a close relative to the Joshua tree, produces a creamy white plume of bell-shaped flowers.**

and picturesque desert flora to Ryan's 5,458-foot summit. At the top, be sure to sign the register, found amid a pile of jagged rocks that geologists estimate to be several hundred million years old. When you return to the trailhead, look for Indian Cave, a rock shelter used by Native Americans, on the parking area's west side. Try to get an early start on this hike — the cooler the temperatures, the more you'll enjoy this trail, which gains 1,000 feet from bottom to top.

## Keys View

Pick a clear morning to visit the drive-up overlook at Keys View, and you'll be treated to a sweeping panorama that takes in two of Southern California's biggest summits: Mount San Jacinto at 10,834 feet, and Mount San Gorgonio at 11,502 feet. Palm Springs and the Coachella Valley frame the background, and the vast Salton Sea shimmers to the southeast. Look carefully and you can pick out the leafy green of the Coachella Valley Preserve's Thousand Palms Oasis directly below you. On the clearest days, keen eyes will spot Signal Mountain in Mexico, more than 90 miles away. Temperatures are always fairly moderate at Keys View, because its elevation is well above 5,000 feet. A short paved trail leads from the parking lot. More ambitious hikers can follow the path to neighboring Inspiration Peak, which offers all the same views but much less company.

## Lost Horse Mine

In a rash of hopefulness in the late 1800s, about 300 mines were dug in what is now Joshua Tree National Park, but only a handful produced

↑ Fortynine Palms Oasis is reached by hiking along the remains of an ancient Native American trail.

↖ Despite being nearly a century old, the stamp mill at Lost Horse Mine has been well preserved in the arid desert air.

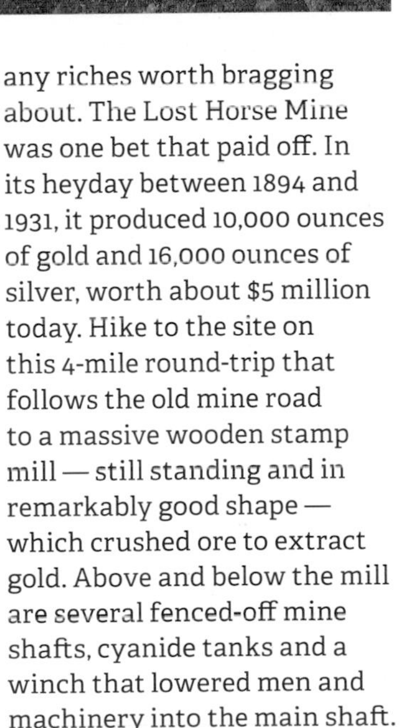

any riches worth bragging about. The Lost Horse Mine was one bet that paid off. In its heyday between 1894 and 1931, it produced 10,000 ounces of gold and 16,000 ounces of silver, worth about $5 million today. Hike to the site on this 4-mile round-trip that follows the old mine road to a massive wooden stamp mill — still standing and in remarkably good shape — which crushed ore to extract gold. Above and below the mill are several fenced-off mine shafts, cyanide tanks and a winch that lowered men and machinery into the main shaft. A grand vista of the park's backcountry can be seen from the top of the ridge, a short distance above the mine.

## Fortynine Palms Oasis

This hike is a showpiece of low-desert flora, including the oasis' namesake 49 palms, a wealth of chubby barrel cacti, and clusters of brittlebush — a shrub with silvery green leaves and a yellow, daisy-like flower. The trail follows sections of an old Native American pathway, climbing up and over a small ridge and then curving around to the

↑ **Joshua Tree's pitch-black skies, far from any city lights, offer nightly opportunities to view the Milky Way arching across the desert sky.**

palm grove, where towering fan palms form a canopy over a trickling spring and clear pools. Like almost all palm oases, this one occurs along a geologic fault line where underground water is forced to the surface. This green, vibrant spot is critically important as a watering hole for bighorn sheep and coyotes. Orioles, finches and hummingbirds also congregate here, especially when the palm fruits ripen.

## Stargazing

On moonless nights, almost any spot in Joshua Tree is good for stargazing. The park's jet-black skies are often clear thanks to the desert's low humidity and distance from light-polluting cities. Even the dimmest of stars can be

spotted with a decent telescope, but your naked eyes alone are enough to render you spellbound under J-Tree's starry skies. Visitors can take advantage of ranger-led night sky programs, typically offered on spring weekends, and just outside the park's Twentynine Palms entrance is Sky's the Limit, a nonprofit observatory and nature center that offers public observing sessions almost every Saturday night. The 15-acre property has its own research observatory, plus an outdoor amphitheater and level pads for amateur astronomers to set up their own equipment. Guests are encouraged to bring binoculars and telescopes, but if you don't have any, another stargazer will most likely be happy to share.

# Joshua Tree National Park Southern Region

***Rugged desert terrain harbors house-sized boulders, a hidden palm oasis, gold mining ruins and a vast cactus field***

## Hot Spot Highlights

- Visit a leafy palm and cottonwood oasis.
- Climb to the top of Mastodon Peak.
- Walk through a garden of jumping cholla cactus.
- Take a class in desert natural history.

**Address**: Cottonwood Spring park entrance (southern entrance); off Interstate 10, 25 miles east of Indio, CA
**Tel.**: (760) 367-5500
**Website**: www.nps.gov/jotr

**Best season:**
October to April

**↗ Deciduous cottonwood trees grow side-by-side with California fan palms at Cottonwood Spring Oasis.**

While northern Joshua Tree National Park contains many of the park's most famous sights, like the Wonderland of Rocks and Ryan Mountain, the park's southern section offers its own rewards — and it's a short drive from Palm Springs, Palm Desert and surrounding communities.

There are no visitor services in the park, so make sure your car is well stocked with gas, snacks and especially water. The large cities of Indio and Palm Desert are about 30 miles west and offer a wide choice of grocery stores, restaurants and lodgings. Cottonwood Spring Campground, near the park's southern entrance, has 62 sites with running water and flush toilets. Sites are available by reservation at www.recreation.gov up to six months in advance of your visit.

## Cottonwood Spring Oasis

This oasis is a little slice of watery paradise for birds and wildlife, and you can see it with only a very short walk. The oasis nourishes not just California fan palms, but also a number of large, leafy cottonwood trees, a species that grows only in constantly wet soil. The Cahuilla Indians used this spring for centuries, and by the 1800s were followed by a succession of prospectors, miners and travelers. Gold mills were built in this area because of the abundance of water. See the bedrock mortars left by the Cahuilla Indians and watch for hummingbirds and hooded orioles flitting near the pools.

## Mastodon Peak

The Mastodon Peak Trail is a pleasant, easy stroll among tall ocotillos, yucca and smaller cacti, punctuated by the oddly shaped, massive rock formations that Joshua Tree is famous for. In only a mile, the trail passes by hundreds of ocotillo plants and a gigantic split boulder — one half lying on the ground and the other standing tall — before

**↑ Joshua Tree's weird and wonderful boulder formations are a playground for hikers, rock climbers and photographers.**

**↖ The view from Mastodon Peak's summit takes in a dramatic sweep of Joshua Tree's southern reaches.**

**↑ The cholla cactus is armed with fishhook-like barbs that look soft and fuzzy but are painfully sharp and difficult to extract from clothing and skin.**

**↑↑ Cottonwood Spring Oasis was an important water stop for early desert travelers, including gold miners, prospectors and teamsters.**

reaching a plateau at the base of Mastodon Peak. This large granite massif is an erosional remnant — a harder rock that withstood the onslaught of wind, water erosion and temperature extremes much better than the softer rocks around it. A quick scramble gets you up to the summit. (Head around the back [east] side for the easiest route.) The sweeping view from the top is rewarding: you see not only a large expanse of Joshua Tree's desert and the Eagle Mountains but also snowcapped Mount San Jacinto and the mirage-like Salton Sea shimmering in the distance some 30 miles away. After you descend from the peak, continue on the main trail to the Mastodon Mine and the Winona Mill Site. The mine was worked in the 1920s with a modicum of success.

## Lost Palms Oasis

Many consider Lost Palms Oasis to be Joshua Tree's best palm grove, and although the hike to reach it is nearly 7 miles round-trip, it has little elevation change. The trail begins at Cottonwood Spring Oasis and meanders through a series of dry washes and low ridges covered with low-elevation desert cacti, mostly barrel cacti and chollas. In spring, you may be treated to a colorful display of flowering shrubs, including red chuparosa, yellow brittlebush and purple indigo bush. Water in the desert always comes as a surprise, but especially so on this trail — you'll see no

← An army of jumping cholla cactus guard the edges of Pinto Basin Road, some reaching higher than six feet.

indication of the huge palm oasis until you are almost on top of it. The main trail brings you to an overlook point above the palms, and a steep use trail descends into the grove, where you can relax under the shade of more than 100 palms, some growing as high as 80 feet tall.

## Cholla Cactus Garden

Jumping cholla cactus is named for its tendency to attach itself to anyone or anything that passes nearby. The spiny cactus doesn't really jump, but fist-sized segments of its branches break off and travel in the wind, allowing the cactus to disperse its seeds. Don't get in a cholla's way on a fiercely windy day — it has more spines per square inch than almost any other cactus, and those spines have fishhook-like barbs that flare out to attach themselves. Needless to say, this plant is a formidable opponent for any herbivore that tries to munch on it, but even so, many birds make their nests in this cactus. Walk through Joshua Tree's roadside Cholla Cactus Garden, a half hour north of Cottonwood Spring on Pinto Basin Road, and you'll be amazed at the photogenic beauty of this seemingly endless collection of densely packed cholla cacti. Their vast numbers seem to go on forever, fading off in the distance at the base of muted purple and tan hills.

## Desert Institute

The Joshua Tree National Park Association runs the Desert Institute, a weekend field program for adults and families that offers courses in natural science, cultural history, creative arts, desert naturalist studies and desert survival. Family programs include half-day classes in animal tracking and using a map and compass. Creative arts programs include writing desert haiku, photographing desert botany and painting watercolors. Science classes focus on lichens, snakes, spiders and other denizens of the desert. Check out the current listing of classes and reserve your spot at www.joshuatree.org.

# Santa Rosa and San Jacinto Mountains National Monument

***Fir-covered alpine slopes, cactus-lined desert canyons and a spectacular aerial tramway define this palms-to-pines park***

## Hot Spot Highlights

- Ride an aerial tramway from palms to pines.
- Hike desert paths high above Palm Springs and Palm Desert.
- See bighorn sheep, roadrunners and other desert creatures.

**Address**: Santa Rosa and San Jacinto Mountains National Monument Visitor Center, 51500 Hwy 74, Palm Desert, CA
**Tel.**: (760) 862-9984
**Websites**: www.blm.gov/visit/santa-rosa-san-jacinto-mountains-national-monument, www.desertmountains.org

**Best season:**
November to April for desert regions
May to October for San Jacinto

↗ **Beavertail cactus are easily identified by their gray-green pads and showy magenta flowers.**

Naturalist and writer John Muir, after ascending Mount San Jacinto, claimed that the view from its summit was "one of the most sublime spectacles seen anywhere on earth." This 10,800-foot granite massif is the crown of the San Jacinto mountain range, which dominates the western skyline above Palm Springs. South of this range is a smaller, lower range — the Santa Rosa Mountains — with Toro Peak and Santa Rosa Peak lording over the horizon. These two ranges and the lesser hills that surround them comprise Santa Rosa and San Jacinto Mountains National Monument.

Far below the peaks lie Palm Springs and neighboring Coachella Valley cities, known for their dry desert climate and brutal

summer temperatures of 115 degrees Fahrenheit. But thanks to the loftiness of the San Jacinto Range, which captures huge amounts of winter rain and snow, the valley is a desert garden spot, filled with palm trees, verdant lawns and golf courses, and spring-fed streams.

You can hike to Mount San Jacinto from Palm Springs via the world-famous Cactus to Clouds Trail, which climbs from the desert floor to the summit with a ludicrous 10,000 feet of elevation gain. Very few attempt this route, and even fewer achieve it. It's so much easier — and far more pleasant — to ride the Palm Springs Aerial Tramway instead. A rotating tram car carries you from palms to pines, or from the desert floor up 6,000 feet in elevation in only 15 minutes. When you disembark at 8,516-foot Mountain Station, you're in a cool alpine forest. In winter, you can cross-country ski or snowshoe in Mount San Jacinto State Park and Wilderness. In summer, choose from a variety of hikes, including the Desert View Trail, an easy walk with mind-expanding vistas every step of the way, especially looking down below to Palm Springs and the Coachella Valley. Mount San Jacinto is known for its spectacular vertical relief, and nowhere is this more apparent than from Desert View.

Ambitious hikers will want to climb from Mountain Station to San Jacinto's summit,

**↑ An icon of the desert, the barrel cactus has an accordion-like skin that can expand to store water after winter rains.**

**↖ Mount San Jacinto's granite massif can be seen from almost everywhere in the northern Coachella Valley — its 10,800-foot summit beckoning desert dwellers to its alpine wonders.**

↑ **Sand verbena, with its spherical bouquets of lavender blossoms, is one of the low desert's most attractive wildflowers.**

↑↑ **The roadrunner is more adept at sprinting than flying, but it will take flight to avoid a predator.**

an 11-mile round-trip through granite-and-fir country. As you walk, be on the lookout for Cooper's hawks and yellow-rumped warblers. Near the top, you'll find a handsome stone hut, built in 1933 by the Civilian Conservation Corps and still used by hikers as an overnight shelter. The peak's awe-inspiring view takes in much of Southern California and parts of Mexico and Nevada.

The alpine hamlet of Idyllwild also offers trail access to Mount San Jacinto State Park and Wilderness, including the 8.4-mile round-trip on Devils Slide Trail to the fire lookout tower on Tahquitz Peak (8,828 feet), one of Southern California's most popular day hikes. A more leisurely hike follows the Ernie Maxwell Scenic Trail out and back from Humber Park, offering fine views of the nearby granite peaks. Hikers who walk any of Idyllwild's trails in May or June may be treated to the glorious sight and beguiling scent of yellow, trumpet-shaped lemon lilies. Coveted for its beauty, the flower was poached to near-extinction in the early 20th century, but a local nonprofit group is working to restore its numbers.

The national monument also has a wide variety of desert trails, many of them with easy access from the Coachella Valley's cities. Treks of any length are possible on the Lykken Trail, which follows the ridgeline above Palm Springs and has several entry and exit points. The trail climbs high above downtown, offering a wilderness-like experience with plentiful desert flora — beavertail and barrel cactus bloom in profusion from March to May — plus expansive desert and city views. This is a great nighttime hike in the warmer months of the year, when you can enjoy the sparkling city lights from high above. In the daytime, keep on the lookout for roadrunners, one of the most beloved birds of the American Southwest. This ferocious hunter and carnivore is known for running at speeds of up to 20 miles per hour. And they don't call "beep-beep" as they zip past — but they do make a rhythmic clucking sound.

Another great Palm Springs hike is the 3.6-mile Garstin/Henderson Loop, which zigzags uphill from a ritzy Palm Springs cul-de-sac, then climbs steeply up Smoketree Mountain and loops downhill through a desert wash. The trail offers close-up charms: multitudes of chubby round barrel cactus line the hillside, and side-blotched lizards perform push-ups on rocks. A longer trek departs the top of Garstin Trail and follows Wildhorse and Clara Burgess Trail to Murray Hill, Palm

Springs' highest summit (2,320 feet). The pointy pinnacle offers a 360-degree vista, with the Salton Sea shimmering in the south and winter-snow-capped Mount San Jacinto framing the west. Much of the Coachella Valley is spread out below you. A few picnic tables provide seating for a view-filled lunch.

In Palm Desert, visitors will find the Santa Rosa and San Jacinto Mountains National Monument Visitor Center, with several trailheads nearby. Desert bighorn sheep are often spotted on many of the monument's trails, especially near oases and springs. This majestic creature is always on the move, despite hauling some heavy baggage — up to 25 pounds of curling horns.

**↑ Both male and female desert bighorn sheep can have horns, but only the male's horns grow long enough to circle backward.**

**↖ Just a few miles from the downtown bustle of Palm Springs, it's easy to find solitude in the protected lands of Santa Rosa and San Jacinto Mountains National Monument.**

# Coachella Valley Preserve

***A fan palm oasis in the middle of the San Andreas fault zone***

## Hot Spot Highlights

- See a desert pond fed by underground springs.
- Look for the Coachella Valley fringe-toed lizard.
- Birdwatch in a fan palm oasis.
- Walk through the San Andreas Fault zone.

**Address**: Coachella Valley Preserve, 29200 Thousand Palms Canyon Road, Thousand Palms, CA
**Tel.**: (760) 343-2733 or (760) 343-1234
**Website**: www.coachellavalleypreserve.org

**Day use only**

**Best season:**
October to April

**↗ The pint-sized burrowing owl makes its home in a hole in the desert sand and, unlike many other owls, is active during the day.**

**→ The Coachella Valley fringe-toed lizard escapes the summer heat by "swimming" or burrowing beneath the sand during peak daylight hours.**

At the 20,000-acre Coachella Valley Preserve, dense groves of California fan palms rise like a leafy mirage from sand and alluvial gravel deposited by the nearby Indio Hills. At this island-in-the-desert, you'll find not only graceful, stately palms but also sand dunes, smoke-tree-lined washes, a pond and marsh, and abundant plant and animal life.

This landscape is bisected by the very active San Andreas Fault zone, which through its frequent shuddering and shaking has caused underground springs to pop up to Earth's surface, giving palm seeds the water they need to germinate. Within the preserve boundaries approximately 1,000 palms provide nourishment and shelter for special desert creatures like the rare southern yellow bat, which nests in the palm "skirts" (dead fronds). But the impetus for the preserve's creation in 1984 was a lizard. The endangered Coachella Valley fringe-toed lizard makes its home only in the Coachella Valley. You'll have to look hard to spot this quick, long-tailed

lizard with "fringes" on its toes, which can dive headfirst into soft sand, leaving no trace for predators to find.

Binoculars are a must at this preserve as the abundant water and shade attract scores of bird species. The hooded oriole weaves its nest on the underside of palm fronds. The great horned owl nests in the treetops. Pint-sized burrowing

owls make their nests in the ground, usually in burrows that have been dug out by ground squirrels or other animals. Western bluebirds, yellow Wilson's warblers, glossy black phainopepla and gray mourning doves are often seen here.

First-time visitors should stop in at the Palm House visitor center — a log cabin constructed from the trunks of palm trees — to get maps and information, then set out on the 4-mile McCallum Trail and Moon Canyon Loop. A raised wooden walkway keeps your feet dry as you wander through the watery marsh of Thousand Palms Oasis, where many of the palms are more than a century old. The trail opens out to a sandy wash that leads to the McCallum Grove, where skirted palms stand sentry over a tranquil pond. Skirt the pond's perimeter, then head uphill on Moon Canyon Trail to gain a ridgetop view of the surrounding Indio Hills.

Several other oases can be visited in the preserve, each with its own charms. During wildflower season (usually March and April), hike the Pushawalla Palms Trail to see a carpet of desert gold blooming along the high ridgetop in the trail's first mile, and purple sand verbena decorating the wash in the trail's last mile.

The nearby city of Palm Springs has numerous options for overnight lodging and dining (www.visitpalmsprings.com).

**↑ Purple sand verbena and desert sunflowers fill the washes with an extravagant color show.**

**↖ Unlike many other palms, California fan palms (*Washingtonia filifera*) retain their "skirts" of dead palm fronds for years, providing habitat for birds, bats and insects.**

# Indian Canyons

***A rugged hiker's paradise of red rock canyons and sulfur streams***

## Hot Spot Highlights

- Hike through the world's largest California fan palm oasis, which harbors more than 80 species of birds.
- See ancient Native American rock art, cactus gardens and towering rock formations.
- Wet your feet at desert waterfalls.

**Addresses**: Indian Canyons, 38500 South Palm Canyon Drive, Palm Springs, CA; Tahquitz Canyon, 500 West Mesquite Avenue, Palm Springs, CA
**Tel.**: Indian Canyons: (760) 323-6018, Tahquitz Canyon: (760) 416-7044
**Websites**: www.indian-canyons.com, www.tahquitzcanyon.com

**Day use only**

**Best season:**
October to April

**↗ The remarkable chuckwalla can wedge itself into a rocky crevice, then blow up the air sac in its belly so no predator can extract it from its hiding place.**

Palm Springs is best known for snowbirds, spring break and "refined" fun — golf courses, spa resorts and tennis courts. But it also has a surprisingly rugged side. Tucked away on the town's southwestern edge are the Indian Canyons: Palm, Andreas, Murray and Tahquitz. In this hiker's paradise, the desert strips off its city clothes and reveals a picturesque landscape of red rock, fan palms, sulfur streams, barrel cacti, bighorn sheep and broad vistas of surprising color and beauty.

The Indian Canyons are part of several thousand acres of reservation land managed by the Agua Caliente tribe, a band of Cahuilla Indians. Backed by the San Jacinto Mountains that tower thousands of feet above the desert floor, the canyons benefit from their high-rising neighbors. Snowmelt runs off these snowcapped peaks into the desert's perennial streams — sometimes only a trickle, sometimes a torrent.

The city of Palm Springs offers all visitor services (www.visitpalmsprings.com).

### Tahquitz Canyon

The four canyons are close together geographically, but each is different in character.

→ **The high peaks of the San Jacinto Range are often snow-covered from December to March, contrasting sharply with the arid desert below.**

↘ **Tahquitz Falls flows vigorously after heavy winter rains and during spring snowmelt in the San Jacinto Mountains.**

Tahquitz Canyon's crystalline creek and lush stands of desert lavender, honey mesquite and leafy sycamores seem almost surreal in Palm Springs' arid climate. Its short loop trail offers an easy hike with a big bonus: its granite and metamorphic rock walls harbor a 60-foot waterfall that runs with remarkable gusto after winter rains. Movie buffs will recognize the showering falls as the entrance to the land of Shangri-La in Frank Capra's 1937 film *Lost Horizon*.

Other treasures of Tahquitz include quartz-laden boulders, red cliffs stained with desert varnish and plentiful bird life. In the canyon's mouth, look for 1,000-year-old Cahuilla Indian rock art, bedrock mortars and ancient irrigation systems. Springtime brings bright-red chuparosa blossoms interspersed with the school-bus yellow of brittlebush on the canyon floor. A well-graded pathway traces alongside the stream. Tahquitz Falls appears like a revelation — a shower of whitewater plummeting over polished granite. The falls are framed by a leafy collection of Fremont cottonwoods and

↑ **Brittlebush blooms along the desert floor for several weeks in spring, its silver leaves upstaged by prolific schoolbus-yellow flowers.**

→ **Beavertail cactus, or *Opuntia basilaris*, offer up one of the desert's most outrageously colorful blooms.**

western sycamores — trees that need their feet in water — thanks to the stream's year-round reliability.

## Palm Canyon

A few miles farther south, Palm Canyon's lush stands of California fan palms extend for nearly 15 miles. This is considered to be the world's largest California fan palm oasis, with many trees reaching 40 feet tall. Footpaths lead through groves of hundred-year-old palms growing so close together that they nearly block out the sun. When Palm Canyon's stream flows with full strength — usually in

the days that follow a heavy winter rain, or during peak snowmelt — you might think you're in the tropics. More often the creek is just a mellow trickle, but on at least a few days each year, it floods high and rushes powerfully enough to close the canyon's access road. Plentiful water and cool palm tree shade attract an

↑ **The rugged red rock of Andreas and Murray canyons stands guard over leafy fan palms and perennial waterways.**

array of wildlife — more than 80 species of birds have been identified in Palm Canyon, including brilliant-yellow hooded orioles and lazuli buntings. Bighorn sheep and coyote come down from the hills to quench their thirst.

## Andreas Canyon and Murray Canyon

In neighboring Andreas Canyon, another year-round stream gives life to more than 150 species of plants. An easy 1-mile loop around the canyon makes an ideal trip for first-time visitors. For a longer trek, hike from Andreas Canyon into palm-shaded Murray Canyon. The canyon gradually narrows into a series of twists and turns, slowly revealing its secrets: 100-foot-high red rock cliffs, stately fan palms with rustling skirts formed by discarded fronds, barrel cacti that grow fat and round after a spring rain, and at trail's end, a beautiful multitiered waterfall called the Seven Sisters. Most of the year, Murray Canyon's stream flows gently, but during wet winters, exercise caution at this trail's stream crossings — the rocks can be slippery and the water deeper than you'd expect. Birders come to Murray Canyon to seek out the endangered least Bell's vireo, which nests amid the palms.

# Mecca Hills Wilderness

***A maze of pastel-hued slot canyons decorated by graceful ocotillos***

### Hot Spot Highlights

- Wander through a colorful labyrinthine canyon.
- Explore water-carved slot canyons and steep sandstone ridges.
- Climb ladders up and over dry waterfalls.

**Address**: Painted Canyon Road, Mecca, CA; in the town of Mecca, take 66th Avenue east for about 4 miles, turn left at the sign for Painted Canyon Road and follow this dirt road for 3.5 miles to the trailhead
**Tel.**: (760) 833-7100
**Website**: www.blm.gov/visit/mecca-hills-wilderness

**Best season:**
October to April

! Road damage may occur after severe storms

↗ **Colorful mineral deposits have brushed the layers of sedimentary rock in Big Painted Canyon with hues of soft pink and gold.**

An hour southeast of Palm Springs, the Mecca Hills Wilderness shelters a maze of pastel-hued slot canyons formed by movement along the San Andreas Fault. This is where two great plates of Earth's crust meet — the Pacific Plate and the North American Plate. In most places, the two plates slip past each other without any interference, but here, the plates collide. Layers of eroded rock, some over 600 million years old, have been pushed up and overturned by this frequent collision.

There are no services in the Mecca Hills, so make sure your car is stocked with gas, food and especially water. Primitive camping is permitted; many campers choose spots alongside Painted Canyon Road. The small town of Mecca has gas and supplies.

## Big Painted Canyon and Ladder Canyon

With an elevation below sea level, the Mecca Hills region is full of geological

→ **Well-placed metal ladders make it possible for hikers to climb up and over dry waterfalls in Ladder Canyon.**

treasures, and they're easy to see on a 5-mile loop up Ladder Canyon and back down Big Painted Canyon.

Both canyons are aptly named. Big Painted Canyon awes and delights with its extraordinary geology and colorful mineral deposits in hues of rose, pink, red, purple and green. The varied palette of colors is attributed to movement on the fault that has brought together sediments from many sources — marine, desert and river. Iron and manganese figure prominently in these rocks' brilliant hues.

Ladder Canyon is pure theme park–style fun. Ordinarily, most casual explorers would be stymied by slick walls, giant boulders and dry waterfalls, but thanks to a series of metal ladders, even casual hikers negotiate this slot canyon. You ascend a ladder, squeeze through a narrow slot between pink and gold sandstone walls, duck your head under a boulder, then climb up another ladder and repeat. The ladders are maintained by a group of local volunteers, but always assess their sturdiness before

climbing or descending.

To connect the two canyons, a trail travels about 1 mile along the rim of the canyon above them. This high mesa is an extraordinary place, especially in spring. The moonscape-like terrain, lined with sparse gravel, is punctuated by hundreds of towering ocotillo plants that frame a long-distance view of the Salton Sea, shimmering to the south. After winter and spring rains, the ocotillos gussy themselves up in bright-red blooms. This iconic desert plant is easy for novices to identify, but serious wildflower hunters search out the rare Mecca aster, a light purple, daisylike blossom.

In its lower reaches, Big Painted Canyon's sandy wash is decorated with ironwood, palo verde and smoke trees.

Smoke trees, so named because they resemble a puff of smoke, are restricted to areas where flash floods occur fairly frequently. Only swirling floodwaters can make the tree's seeds germinate.

## Box Canyon Road Trailheads

Several other trailheads are accessible off Box Canyon Road beyond the Painted Canyon Road turnoff. Drive 3.4 miles past Painted Canyon Road to reach the trailhead for so-called Never Ending Canyon, another relatively easy loop hike through two narrow, colorful canyons. Adventurous hikers with good navigational skills may want to tackle The Grottos (the trailhead is at Sheep Hole Oasis, 5 miles past the Painted Canyon Road turnoff). Here, two slot canyons have been filled with giant boulders, creating caves that can be explored with a headlamp or flashlight. It's also a smart idea to wear a helmet, just in case you misjudge how tall you are.

**↑ The furrowed ridges and valleys of the Mecca Hills are surrounded by miles of sandy desert washes.**

**↖ The iconic ocotillo plant is revered for its bright red blooms, which attract hummingbirds and other pollinators.**

**← The Salton Sea appears like a distant mirage beyond the folds and creases of the Mecca Hills.**

# Anza-Borrego Desert State Park Northern Region

***California's largest state park delivers watery oases, kaleidoscopic wildflower displays and intriguing geologic features***

## Hot Spot Highlights

- Hike to a leafy oasis of fan palms.
- Squeeze your way through a narrow slot canyon.
- Be dazzled by the night sky.
- Get wowed by wildflowers.
- View the Carrizo Badlands at sunset or sunrise.

**Address**: Anza-Borrego Desert State Park, 200 Palm Canyon Drive, Borrego Springs, CA
**Tel.**: (760) 767-4205 or (760) 767-5311
**Websites**: www.parks.ca.gov/anzaborrego, theabf.org, www.abdnha.org

**Best season:**
October to April

↗ **A remnant of an earlier, wetter epoch, California fan palms are confined to a few stream- or spring-fed canyon oases, such as Borrego Palm Canyon.**

This dually named park commemorates Juan Bautista de Anza, the Spanish explorer who traveled across the desert in 1774, and the majestic bighorn sheep or *borrego*, which roams the ridges and canyons. Crowning California's park system with the largest tract of state-preserved land, Anza-Borrego Desert spans more than 600,000 acres of badlands, palm oases, slot canyons, sandy washes and cactus gardens. But this huge chunk of untrammeled earth isn't fixed in place. It's a geology lesson in process, constantly moving and changing shape from earthquakes, flash floods and erosion.

### Borrego Palm Canyon

Start your trip at the park's Borrego Palm Canyon visitor center — built underground

↑ A kaleidoscopic wildflower show brightens the sandy washes each year, usually beginning in late February or early March.

for cooling efficiency — to check on current conditions of park roads and trails. Then take the 3-mile round-trip trek into neighboring Borrego Palm Canyon, a watery haven fed by underground springs and shaded by magnificent California fan palms, the only native California palm tree. A remnant of an earlier, wetter epoch, today these palms are found only in a few spring- or stream-fed desert oases. This is the largest of the park's more than 25 fan palm groves, but it's smaller than it used to be. A severe rainstorm and flash flood in 2004 wiped out dozens of Borrego Palm Canyon's oldest palms — you'll see their trunks scattered about the canyon. The intense rain created a wall of water 30 feet high and 100 feet wide that sent witnesses running for their lives. (Meanwhile, not a single drop of rain fell in the town of Borrego Springs, only 3 miles away. Such are the vagaries of desert storms.)

The trail begins in a sandy, rocky wash lined with ocotillo and massive boulders and delivers you to a shady oasis where you can listen to the desert breeze rustle the palm fronds, and in the wetter months, dip your feet in a cool pool. Listen and

↑ **Blue-purple phacelia minor (desert canterbury bells) look innocent enough, but the hairs on its stems and leaves give some people a skin rash.**

↑↑ **Bright pink Bigelow's monkeyflower bloom in sandy gravel washes.**

↗ **The mighty bighorn sheep never sheds its horns, which continue to grow as the animal ages and can weigh up to 30 pounds — more than all the bones in its body combined.**

watch for bird life — more than 80 migratory species use this oasis as a watering stop. Bighorn sheep also come here to drink, especially in the dawn and dusk hours.

## Spring Wildflowers

Anza-Borrego's busiest season is spring, when a wealth of wildflowers brightens the desert sand. If the winter rains have worked their magic, more than 200 flowering plant species put on a brilliant display from late February to late April. In the most productive years, knee-high fields of annual flowers rise out of the sandy desert floor. But the amount, quality and exact location of the peak bloom varies from year to year, so serious flower lovers keep tabs on the park's website for up-to-date information on timing and locations (or phone the recorded wildflower hotline, [760] 767-4684). Even in merely average years, expect to see patches of yellow brittlebrush, purple desert lavender, tall and spiky red ocotillos, and purple sand verbena on the desert floor and along the roadsides. Blooming barrel cactus and yucca color the higher elevations. Borrego Palm Canyon is a reliable starting point for flower seekers. A more ambitious hike leads into Hellhole Canyon and offers rewards of flowering barrel cactus, lupine and phacelia, plus cascading water at 20-foot-high Maidenhair Falls (a 5.6-mile round-trip). Four-wheeling flower fans can scope out the pink sand

↑ **The desert-hardy ocotillo can soar to 30 feet high. A few days after a rain, its thorny stems produce bright green leaves.**

verbena and dune evening primrose on the Coyote Canyon Road, a dirt road at the north end of DiGiorgio Road (two-wheel-drive cars can make the trip but turn around at Desert Gardens about 1.7 miles in). This region often has large displays of desert lilies, recognizable by their heavenly scent. Another great place to see lilies — along with brown-eyed primroses and hairy desert sunflowers — is in the sandy wash off Henderson Canyon Road.

## Font's Point

Visitors with four-wheel-drive vehicles should not miss the chance to visit Font's Point at sunset. During the golden hour, the Borrego Badlands' creased and wrinkled ridges cast bold shadows across a maze of golden hills and sand-colored arroyos. Also known as California's Grand Canyon, Font's Point is a photographer's delight, but getting there means negotiating 4 miles of primitive, sandy, rutted road. If your car isn't suitably equipped, stick to the pavement and get a long-distance view of the park's southernmost badlands at Carrizo Badlands Overlook (on the east side of County Road S-2).

## The Slot

Geology buffs and kids of almost any age find their fun at the Slot, where Anza-Borrego's geologic landscape has been sliced open by time and water. An easy walk through the Slot's narrow siltstone canyon shows off a cross section of brayed tan earth, dissected by nature's forces. From the parking area, the trail descends into a 30-foot-deep crevice. The canyon quickly narrows as you head downhill, and you'll squeeze through walls that constrict to shoulder width. A half mile in is a gravity-defying natural bridge — a boulder precariously lodged in a narrow gap. Where the canyon widens and meets up with a jeep road, you can loop back by climbing to the canyon rim, or just turn around and retrace your steps. (Trailhead is on Buttes Pass Road west of Ocotillo Wells, 2 miles from Highway 78. The dirt road is navigable by passenger cars.)

## Stargazing

Within the park's boundaries lies the unpretentious town of Borrego Springs, population 3,500, the only California town that is completely surrounded by a state park. The city is an official International Dark Sky Community — the first in California — and its citizenry are dedicated to protecting the

night sky from light pollution. The local airport adjusted its aircraft beacon to angle downward, and the town has retrofitted light fixtures and replaced bright lights with more dark-sky-friendly amber lights to create less light pollution. Anza-Borrego regularly offers night sky interpretive programs. Monthly stargazing and moon-watching programs allow visitors to learn about features of the night sky, the importance of darkness and the steps the park is taking to protect dark skies. Check the park website for a current calendar. Or just pick any spot in the park to lay out a blanket at night, and you'll be treated to a grand show of the Milky Way.

Much of Anza-Borrego Desert State Park is accessible only via primitive roads or on foot, so visitors driving two-wheel-drive passenger cars should check for updates on dirt road conditions. The park has four developed campgrounds (reserve online at www.reservecalifornia.com or phone [800] 444-7275). The most popular is Borrego Palm Canyon Campground near the park visitor center. Primitive backcountry camping is also permitted throughout the park (no fees; no reservations). The small town of Borrego Springs has several motels, B&Bs and restaurants. For a luxurious overnight stay, book a room at La Casa del Zorro Resort or the Borrego Valley Inn. For breakfast or lunch, head to Red Ocotillo.

**↑ Borrego Springs was named as California's first International Dark Sky Community for its efforts to minimize light pollution and preserve the brilliance of the desert's night sky.**

**← A trip through the Slot is a chance to explore the earth's belly, its surface sliced open by rushing water and time.**

# Anza-Borrego Desert State Park Southern Region

***The park's southern region is home to fossilized sea shells, lush cactus gardens, water-storing trees and 1,000-year-old indigenous art***

### Hot Spot Highlights

- Explore the Wind Caves' wind-sculpted rock formations.
- Examine ancient Native American pictographs.
- Marvel at the remains of a remote desert homestead.
- See the aptly named elephant tree.
- Hike to six hidden palm oases.

**Address**: Anza-Borrego Desert State Park, 200 Palm Canyon Drive, Borrego Springs, CA
**Tel.**: (760) 767-4205 or (760) 767-5311
**Websites**: www.parks.ca.gov/anzaborrego, theabf.org, www.abdnha.org

**Best season:**
October to April

**↗ The sandstone Wind Caves were used as shelters by Native Americans.**

## Wind Caves

Get a close look at Anza-Borrego's amazing geology at the Wind Caves off Split Mountain Road near Ocotillo Wells. The 4.3-mile dirt road to the trailhead is a spectacular trip through tall, colorful canyon walls formed by layered sediments from ancient lakebeds. Anza-Borrego's geologic story revolves around water: fossilized sea shells prove that most of this desert was once submerged under both tropical waters from the Gulf of California and fresh water from the Colorado River. Animals like sea turtles and sharks once swam in what is now parched desert. The scenic drive is reward enough (a four-wheel-drive vehicle is recommended), but once you reach the trailhead, a steep three-quarter-mile hike provides sweeping views of a prominently striped mud hill formation known as Elephant Knees. The trail then deposits you at the sandstone Wind Caves. It's easy to see

↑ **After a rain, the elephant tree's trunks swell up with stored water.**

why early Native Americans used these "holes in the rock" as natural shelters — many of the alcoves are large enough for a small family.

## Elephant Tree Trail

On your return drive from the Wind Caves, take a short side-trip off Split Mountain Road to the Elephant Tree Trailhead. Also known as "torote," this odd-looking tree is fairly common in Mexico, but much rarer in the United States. Its stout, branching, elephant-like trunk swells up to store water and gives the tree its name, but its beauty lies in its star-shaped cream flowers and aromatic red fruit. The tree, which gives off a spicy, pine-like aroma, was revered by Cahuilla Native Americans for its red sap, said to cure diseases. Early desert settlers and prospectors told stories of finding elephant trees in remote parts of Anza-Borrego desert, but most botanists were skeptical. In 1937, their existence was finally verified by scientists from the San Diego Natural History Museum. The 1.5-mile Elephant Tree Trail takes you past a single fine specimen of the tree and also shows off a good sampling of

↑ **The nomadic Kumeyaay Indians drew colorful rock art on boulders in Blair Valley, but their meaning remains a mystery.**

↗ **Stately ocotillo plants punctuate the sparse, sandy terrain of southern Anza-Borrego. Each plant may live for up to a century.**

Anza-Borrego's common flora: creosote bush, burrobush, indigo bush, cheesebush, cat's claw, smoke tree and more.

## Blair Valley Area

When the temperatures heat up in Anza-Borrego, head for Blair Valley, where the elevations are higher and the air temperature is typically 10 degrees cooler. For a short and easy hike, go see the Native American rock art on the Pictograph Trail in Little Blair Valley. The drawings — a series of zigzag lines and diamond shapes painted in red and yellow pigments — are found on a large boulder on the trail's right side, less than a mile from the start. Most likely the rock art was the work of nomadic Kumeyaay Indians, possibly dating back 1,000 years. Archaeologists are not sure what the drawings were intended to convey.

Also in Blair Valley are the silent ruins of one man's dream. Take a 1-mile uphill hike to the top of Ghost Mountain to see the crumbling remains of Marshal South's utopian vision — the 1930s homestead that South, his wife Tanya and their three children shared for 17 years. Australian-born South, a talented poet and artist, lived in the desert's harsh extremes by emulating the spartan style of early Native Americans. On this remote desert hilltop, South and his family built an adobe home, invented systems for storing precious rainfall, grew a vegetable garden and harvested seeds and fruits from desert plants. To earn money, South wrote magazine articles about his back-to-nature lifestyle, inspiring a

↑ **At Palm Bowl Grove, more than 100 fan palms offer respite from the desert sun. The Cahuilla Indians made sandals, baskets and thatched roofs from their fibers.**

following of loyal, fascinated readers. South's wife eventually grew weary of her husband's odd idealism and their rugged life, and the family split up and left the mountain in 1948. All that remains are a few partial adobe walls, an old mattress frame, a few cisterns and barrels, and a thriving desert garden of ocotillo, yucca and barrel cactus.

## Mountain Palm Springs Loop

This hike offers the chance to linger under the shimmering fronds of shady palm trees in six separate oases, each less than a mile apart. Hike only a couple of miles to see one or two oases, or as much as 6.5 miles to see them all. Because of this grove's more remote location, you'll have much less human company here than you'll find at the oasis at Borrego Palm Springs Canyon. Head straight at the trailhead sign to walk the loop's south side first, visiting the small Pygmy Grove and larger Southwest Grove, or take the right fork to walk the north side first, visiting Mary's Grove, North Grove and Surprise Canyon Grove. Both trails connect at Surprise Canyon Grove, where a side trail travels to Palm Bowl Grove, the largest in this area. Here, an array of more than 100 stately palms grow in an amphitheater-like basin. (The trail begins at Mountain Palm Springs Campground, less than a mile from Highway S-2.)

Primitive camping is allowed at Mountain Palm Springs Campground, and a developed campground is located at Bow Willow. For more details, see Anza-Borrego Northern Region (pages 242–7).

# Index

Text in **bold** type refers to major hot spot entries all of which are extensively illustrated. Numbers in **bold** type refer to photographs of the item indexed.

# Photo Credits

All photos © Ann Marie Brown except as listed below.

Bureau of Land Management (BLM)
- Bob Wick: 61 (bottom right), 98, 99, 100, 101 (bottom right), 215 (top), 241
- David Ledig: 54, 55 (top), 55 (middle right), 56

Channel Islands National Park: 181

Hartley Millson: 2–3

Lava Beds National Monument: 14

National Park Service: 12, 29, 31, 32, 33, 87 (bottom right), 132, 166, 168, 172, 179 (bottom), 186, 187 (top), 188, 189

Shutterstock.com
- Ajinkya9: 46 (bottom)
- Alberto Loyo: 35
- Anatoliy Lukich: 78
- Anton Foltin: 203 (bottom right), 243
- Bill Kennedy: 97
- Birdiegal: 22 (bottom left)
- BlaineT: 240 (top)
- Bonnie Fink: 149 (bottom)
- Brian Lasenby: 150 (bottom)
- Bridget Calip: 8–9, 207
- Cameron Aumann: 193 (left)
- Chad McDermott: 159 (right)
- Christopher Boswell: 15
- Clayton Harrison: 182–83
- Colin D. Young: 105 (bottom)
- Collins93: 68 (bottom)
- David Litman: 82–83 (top)
- Diane N. Ennis: 19
- digidreamgrafix: 61 (middle left), 68 (top)
- dlhca: 191
- Doug Meek: 96 (top)
- Enrique Aguirre: 66 (bottom)
- Esposito Photography: 173
- Esterelv: 200
- Foto 4440: 192 (bottom)
- Frank Fennema: 106 (middle left)
- Irina Mos: 244 (top right)
- Jane Rix: 126
- Jason Mintzer: 187 (bottom)
- Jeffrey B. Banke: 150–51 (top)
- Jerry S: 69 (top)
- Joe Morris 917: 80, 201 (top left)
- Karel Stipek: 221 (right)
- Kavram: 174 (top)
- Kim Grosz: 240 (bottom)
- Kit Leong: 101 (top), 171
- kojihirano: 34
- Kyle T. Perry: 185 (top left)
- LA Nature Graphics: 193 (right)
- Lost_in_the_Midwest: 95 (top)
- Lowe Llaguno: 195 (top)
- Lucky-photographer: 175, 201 (bottom right)
- Lynn Yeh: 92
- Maddy M: 17
- Max Allen: 148
- Meganopierson: 161 (bottom)
- Ofe Martinez: 27 (top left)
- Patrick Poendl: 146 (bottom), 154–55 (top)
- Phitha Tanpairoj: 61 (bottom left), 93
- Ranchorunner: 16
- rbrown10: 96 (bottom)
- Robert Kothenbeutel: 47 (bottom)
- Robert Loe: 202 (bottom), 222–23
- Robert Mutch: 28
- Sebastian Burel: 184, 185 (middle left)
- Stephen Moehle: 116 (left)
- steve estvanik: 199 (bottom left)
- Sundry Photography: 70, 74
- Terence: 81 (top)
- Thomas Tichy: 147 (middle left), 161 (top)
- Tim Zurowski: 179 (top), 180
- TomKli: 6–7, 130
- Tom Reichner: 24 (top left), 104 (right)
- Tom Tietz: 190
- turtix: 170
- Wollertz: 125, 206
- Xiu Yu Photography: 247
- Zack Frank: 13 (right)

Front cover: © Tim Fitzharris

Back cover (top to bottom): Bridget Calip/Shutterstock.com; rbrown10/Shutterstock.com; Phitha Tanpairoj/Shutterstock.com